D0375596

BY
SEARCHING

My Journey Through
Doubt Into Faith

ISOBEL KUHN

MOODY PRESS

CHICAGO

© China Inland Mission
(Now known as the Overseas Missionary Fellowship)
American Edition, 1959
ISBN 0-8024-0053-1

Moody Press, a ministry of the Moody Bible Institute, is
designed for education, evangelization and edification.
If we may assist you in knowing more about Christ and
the Christian life, please write us without obligation to:
Moody Press, c/o MLM, Chicago, Illinois 60610.

45 47 49 50 48 46

Printed in the United States of America

CONTENTS

THE QUESTION THAT PIERCED THE MIST
"Canst thou *by searching* find out God?"—Job 11:7

THE ANSWER
Ye shall *seek* me, and *find* me, when ye shall search for me with all your heart.—Jer. 29:13

Jesus said unto him, *I am the way,* the truth, and the life; no man cometh unto the Father, but by me.—John 14:6

Search the Scriptures . . . they are they which testify of me.—John 5:39

If any man will do his will, he shall know of the doctrine, whether it be of God.—John 7:17

CHAPTER ONE

ON TO THE MISTY FLATS

To every man there openeth
A way, and ways, and a way.
And the high soul climbs the high way,
And the low soul gropes the low.
And in between on the misty flats
The rest drift to and fro.
But to every man there openeth
A high way and a low—
And every man decideth the way his soul shall go
—JOHN OKENHAM

O F COURSE no one in this enlightened age believes any more in the myths of Genesis and—" But here Dr. Sedgewick paused in his lecture as if a second thought had occurred. With a twinkle in his eye, he said, "Well, maybe I had better test it out, before being so dogmatic." Facing the large freshman class, who were hanging on his words, and pulling his face into gravity, he asked: "Is there anyone here who believes there is a Heaven and a Hell? Who believes that the story of Genesis is true? Please raise your hand." He waited for a response.

Up went my hand as bravely as I could muster courage. I also looked around to see if I had a comrade in my stand. Only one other hand was up, in

5

all that big group of perhaps a hundred students. Dr. Sedgewick smiled, then, as if sympathetic with our embarrassment, he conceded: "Oh, you just believe that because your papa and mama told you so." He then proceeded with his lecture, assuming once and for all that no thinking human being believed the Bible any more.

Brought up in an earnest Presbyterian home (my grandfather was a Presbyterian minister and my father an ardent lay preacher) I had been carefully coached in the refutations of modernism before my parents had allowed me to enter the university. If it had been a case of arguing the claims of modernism versus fundamentalism, I do not think I would have been shattered in my faith. But there was no argument. There was just the pitying sneer, "Oh, you just believe that because your papa and your mama told you so," and then the confident assumption that no persons nowadays who thought for themselves, who were scientific in their approach to life, believed that old story any more.

On the way home from class I faced the charge honestly. *Why* did I believe the Bible? The Genesis explanation of life's origin? Why did I believe in Heaven and Hell?

It was because I had been taught it by my parents and church from the hour I could understand anything. Was that reason enough for accepting it? No, I agreed with Dr. Sedgewick that it was not a sufficient basis to build my life upon. We had experienced remarkable answers to prayer in our family life—didn't that prove the existence of God? But my psychology course taught that mind had a powerful effect over matter. If I had not been so gullible, maybe I could have seen a natural explanation. Our twentieth century believed only when there was a test and a proof. We were scientific in our investigations; we did not swallow the superstitions of our ancestors just because they were handed to us.

Dr. Sedgewick, Professor of the English Department in our university, was an ardent follower of Matthew Arnold's "sweetness and light" philosophy, and of Thomas Hardy's materialism. Yet he was so apparently patient and kind toward us whom he felt were still bound by our parents' old-fashioned thinking that he won our affection and respect.

At the end of my walk home, I came to the conclusion that I would henceforth accept no theories of life which I had not proved personally. And, quite ignorant of where that attitude would lead me, I had unconsciously stepped off the High Way where man walks with his face lifted Godward and the pure, piney scents of the Heights call him upward, on to The Misty Flats. The in-between level place of easygoing—nothing very good attempted, yet nothing bad either—where men walk in the mist, telling each other that no one can see these things clearly. The Misty Flats where the in-betweeners drift to and fro— life has no end but amusement and no purpose— where the herd drift with the strongest pull and there is no reason for opposing anything. Therefore they had a kind of peace and a mutual link which they call tolerance.

I did not know that I had stepped down to The Misty Flats. I was just conscious of a sudden pleasant freedom from old duties. If there was no God, why bother to go to church on Sunday, for instance? Why not use Sunday to catch up on sleep, so that one could dance half the night away several times during the week?

Again, if the Bible was but a record of myths and old-fashioned ideas, why read it every morning? That took time and it was much easier to sleep until the very last moment, getting up just in time for the first class at college. Prayer, too, became silly—talking to someone who maybe did not exist.

I would not call myself an atheist because, well, there were those childhood answers to prayer still to be accounted for. But I called myself an agnostic —I frankly did not know if there was a God or not. It was a popular thing to be on The Misty Flats: you had plenty of company. And one was respected as being modern and intelligent to question the old faiths. Life drifted along so pleasantly—*for a while*.

My home training still had an effect upon me. Jesus Christ, now seen blurred in the mists which denied His Godhead, is an acknowledged historical character. And His name was still an ointment poured forth to me. He was like a perfume which haunts and calls so that one stops, lifts one's head and drinks it in wistfully. His name was the sweetest melody I knew and it never failed to stir my heart, even though I had ceased to seek Him. His purity and holiness made me hate besmirching things.

And all this because my father and my mother had taught me so.

So when I broke with the old religious habits and frankly went into the world, I was still choosey in what I did. I never smoked. The tainted breath and stained fingers or teeth of the smoker revolted me. I told myself I was too dainty for such doings.

Neither did I drink. My father, brokenhearted at my callous turning-of-the-back on all my home training, still warned me as a medical man what drink could do to a girl.

"Drink affects men and women biologically, and under its influence girls can be led into sin that they could never consent to when in possession of their senses. Dr. Hall and I have such come to us for consultation all the time. They never meant to, but there they are. Keep away from liquor and you can keep yourself pure, perhaps." So I did not drink. Also I had *signed the pledge* when twelve years old, and a certain whimsical loyalty to my childhood self kept me from breaking it.

So amidst the gay group at the university I was considered *a good girl,* and even a Christian! But I myself knew that I wasn't.

In my studies I took the honors course in English Language and Literature which brought me much under the influence of Dr. Sedgewick. But in my extracurricular activities I was mostly interested in the Players Club, the amateur theatrical club of the university. Apparently I had a gift for acting comedy parts, and in my freshman year I won life-membership in the Players Club, not usually attained by a first-year student. The staff patron of our theatricals was Professor H. G. C. Wood, also a member of the English Faculty. He was a believer in God and Christ, and not an atheist like Dr. Sedgewick, and his friendship helped to keep me from extremes. But the theater was his hobby and soon became mine. Urgently my mother pleaded with me to attend the Young Women's Christian Association. I went several times, but was frankly bored, so dropped it. I loved the theater and I liked to dance and these activities occupied my spare time. In fact, our Varsity 1922 yearbook has, as comment opposite my picture: "And oh the tilt of her heels when she dances!" No shadow of the missionary there.

In my second year I was elected to be Secretary of the Student Council, at that time the highest position to which a woman student could be elected. I met the leading young people of the university and became secretly engaged to Ben, one of the star Rugby and basketball players.

Ben was a returned soldier from World War I, several years older than I, not handsome, but six feet two or three in height. He came of a good Baptist family and my mother encouraged our friendship. He even took me to his church on Sunday nights! It made a nice inexpensive date, for Ben did not have much money and when he asked me to marry him he said that our engagement must be kept secret lest his "old man" be angry with him for getting involved before he graduated. I insisted that my parents be told, but his never were. We went together for nearly two years, and my path was perceptibly downgrade.

CHAPTER TWO

SLIPPERY WAYS IN DARKNESS

Wherefore their way shall be unto them as slippery ways in the darkness: they shall be driven on, and fall therein: for I will bring evil upon them, even the year of their visitation, saith the Lord.

Jer. 23:12

AFTER THE STRETCHED MUSCLES of climbing, to find oneself on the level is very relaxing and pleasant. Therefore The Misty Flats are attractive to foot, eye, and palate *at the beginning*. There is no hint that the pretty mist will gradually close in and bring darkness. There is no suggestion amid the gay chatter of the populous throng that there are slippery places, which are going to bring hurt. In the boasted freedom of drifting whither you will, there is certainly no sign that one is being *driven on,* as Jeremiah so shrewdly perceived was the reality. And above all, there is never a hint that the end of The Flats is the visitation of the Lord and the judgment of sin. Yet all that is the real truth.

In my senior year there came a day when my college chum, Cora, shook me to the foundations with a sentence or so. "Isobel," she said, "I think I should tell you something, even though it may hurt. Every-

11

body but you knows that Ben is not loyal to you. He is taking Reba out behind your back."

I turned a stunned face upon her, and her eyes filled with tears of sympathy, but with true friendship she went on: "You remember when you were ill and could not go to his fraternity dance?"

"Yes," I replied, "he took Reba in my place that night. He asked me if I would mind, and I said no."

"Well, that was the beginning of it, I guess. They've been seen together a lot. People are talking and I can't bear that you should not know. I don't think he's worth breaking your heart over, Isobel," she said earnestly.

But it did break my heart. It was difficult to believe and yet I knew he had not been so attentive of late. My father had spoken to me about it. "You have let Ben get too sure of you, Baby," he had said, using his tender pet name for me, the youngest in the family. "Show a man all the love you have *after you are married,* but keep it in reserve while you are just engaged. The elemental male *likes* to fight for a mate. What is the use of chasing a streetcar after you've caught it?"

So it was not all Ben's fault. I had been inexperienced—I was still only in my teens. With the promise 'o be his wife I had truly given my heart to Ben and love struggled hard with "maybe if I . . ." and "perhaps I could still win him back." But it was Ben himself who made it hopeless.

I met him one morning at the entrance of the university. No one else was around, so I charged him with taking Reba out behind my back. I wanted to hear from his own lips that it was true, for love rebelled at believing it. He drew himself up to the full stature of his six feet two inches, and I never forgot the curl of his lip as he said, "Isobel, you're a softy. You don't suppose, do you, that after we are married, I'm not going to take other women out sometimes?"

"Then we part," I had whispered hoarsely, dazed as if stricken. I was on my way home from a class and have never forgotten the dull agony of that walk. I knew I could never marry a man with such standards. That was the trouble. They were just the standards of The Misty Flats. But I had known the Christ and I could not be satisfied with less than the ideals He had set before me.

So I found myself in the slippery places of darkness. Pride wounded me, love wounded me, and sleep departed from me. The English course I was taking entailed more work than a mere passing degree, and I needed rest during sleep hours, but could not sleep.

My mother was distressed that I should break with Ben and kept saying, "If you would only take my advice." But I could not bear to discuss it with anyone. I discussed it with myself night and day. My father was my greatest comfort. He knew enough to be silent and just love me. He even sensed that I was not sleeping. One night when all the house had been asleep for hours and I was still tossing, I heard him come softly into my room. He knelt down beside my bed and prayed God to help me, but it only irritated me. "Thanks, Dad," I said wearily. "I know you mean it well, but praying doesn't go beyond the ceiling, you know." I never forgot the groan with which he turned away from my agnosticism, and left the room.

The climax came just before Christmas. My birthday is December 17 and I was to be twenty years old, but I do not remember if it was before or after that date. The post office clock on Main Street had just struck two, and I was still tense and tossing. I was desperate. I knew I'd be ill in the morning if I did not get to sleep. Then came the Tempter.

"Of what use is life?" he whispered. "Ben is only an average fellow. Probably all men are just like him. You'll never find anyone to love you like you want to be loved—your ideal is too high. And you'd never be happy with a lower ideal of marriage. Why go on with life? It has no purpose, only suffering. This would be a good time to slip out. There is that bottle in the bathroom marked *Poison*. A good long drink and your troubles are over." A good idea. The only sensible solution. I jumped out of bed and started for the bathroom. *Slippery ways in the darkness: they shall be driven on and fall therein.*

My hand was on the door knob when a deep groan, twice repeated, broke the silence of the dark. It was my father, moaning in his sleep in the next room. I was not afraid, for I recognized Father's tones, but I was startled into remembrance of him. I stood with my hand on the knob debating. If I committed suicide, Daddy would think I had gone to Hell. Of course, that would not make a place called Hell, but how terrible for Daddy to think so. He had been such a dear, kind father to me all my life. Dare I make him such a dastardly return? No, I couldn't be so mean and selfish. In agony I turned and sat down on the edge of my bed and faced the darkest moment of my life. I didn't want to live and I couldn't die! Oh the black despair of The Misty Flats! How little did I know of the golden sunshine pouring on the High Way above them! What a lot of heartache I might have been saved if I had only been told that

God had already laid His hand on one who was to be a dear husband to me with the same ideals and the same passion for God's highest purposes! But it was necessary that first I drink to the dregs the emptiness of the promises held out by The Misty Flats: only then could I be freed from their lure and subtle call.

And now a strange thing happened. That day I had been studying Matthew Arnold's essay on *The Study of Poetry*. (You remember, it was Sedgewick, a disciple of Arnold, who had first pushed me off the High Way?) In that essay he gives various quotations from the classics as touchstones of perfect poetry. One such was from Dante and ran: *In la sua volontade ē nostra pace*. From my knowledge of Latin I had guessed the meaning: *In His will is our peace*. Now that sentence wrote itself across the dark of my bedroom. Dante believed in God. What if there were a God, after all? If so, I certainly had not been in His will. Maybe that was why I had no peace? An idea struck me. No one was watching to see if I were a fool or not. Sitting there on my bed's edge, I raised both hands heavenward. "God, if there be a God," I whispered, for I was not going to believe in what did not exist just to get a mental opiate, "if You will prove to me that You are, and if You will give me peace, I will give You my whole life. I'll do anything You ask me to do, go where You send me, obey You all my days." Then I climbed into bed and pulled the blankets over me.

CHAPTER THREE

WHAT YOU SHOULD NOT
IMITATE

THE NEXT THING I KNEW, it was morning and the golden sunshine of a December day in Vancouver was pouring into my bedroom. I lay there drowsily enjoying it when suddenly a thought startled me into full consciousness. I had been sleeping like a baby— how did it happen? Such deep relaxed slumber had not touched my pillow for many a long day. What had brought it? Thought traced itself back to the experience of the night before. I had made a bargain with God. I had asked Him for peace and—*peace had come*. Oh yes, answered Reason; but that was easily explainable apart from God. That was no proof that God existed. It was just the effect of mind over matter. I had committed my troubles to an imaginary being and that was why body and mind quietened down.

Restlessly I threw off the bedclothes and sat on the edge of my bed. I was not going to use religion as an opiate. I was going to be realistic or nothing— as a matter of fact, I believe I was born with "a flair for reality." But as I pondered, the thought persisted: "You made a bargain last night. The

Other Side kept His part. There was no stipulation as to how peace should come, *and it came*. Nobody knows about it and nobody will know, if this should prove to be foolishness. Why not continue your part of the agreement and see?"

But what was *my part?* To yield my whole life *if* He proved Himself. And in the meantime, why not try to seek Him?

Seek God? Where?

Can a man by searching find out God? Zophar had questioned Job, obviously not believing it possible. Job had tried to answer by pointing to God in His creative works. But the twentieth century had another theory for the origin of the earth.

Where does one go to search for God? Even as I asked myself that question, a picture from memory floated before me. It was at the Guelph conference of 1921 when the Student Christian Movement was formed. A young man was on his feet giving his testimony. "While I was interned in Germany as a prisoner of war," he said, "I got hold of a Bible and started to read it. *I found God through reading His Word."*

I had been a university delegate for the Y.W.C.A. to that convention, but had apparently been unaffected by it. I knew there was a conflict between the modernist students and the fundamentalists—this young ex-soldier was earnest for the old beliefs. I was still an agnostic and weary of religious arguments. I let them talk and did not let it enter my heart. But this young fellow was aglow with something real: he was the outstanding memory of that conference to me, yet I did not even know his name. Now in my own hour of need I could see him standing there, radiant, affirming he had *found God*. And

he had found Him through the Christ of the New
Testament.

Well, I had a Bible. There it was on my bookshelf,
unused, a bit dusty, but beautiful and new—a gift
from my father when I graduated from high school.
I pulled it down and looked at it. Modernists said
the Pentateuch was not written by Moses; this was
questioned, that was questioned. Was there anything that wasn't questioned? Yes—the historicity
of Jesus Christ is beyond doubt. And the four Gospels are accepted as a more or less authentic record
of His teachings, as authoritative as Plato's were of
Socrates, at least.

So I decided to search for God *through Jesus
Christ,* to read the Gospels only, to underline everything and anything that Jesus said *to do* and try
honestly to do them. Jesus prayed, so I would begin
to try praying again—cautiously, of course, and not
really assuming that it went any higher than the ceiling. With that decided, I arose and dressed for another day's study at the University of British Columbia.

And now began a life at two levels: an outer level
of study, worldly gaiety and pride, and an inner level
of watching, seeking after God—if there was a God
(always I added that).

God is not a puppet. Man may not pull strings
and expect Him to perform—not even doctrinally
correct strings, such as Balaam tried to pull. God
is not man's servant, that a puny atheist may shout
a challenge and He is bound to respond. Neither
is God a genie, that if man is lucky enough to find
the right combination of words, He will suddenly
pop out and reveal Himself. God is our Creator, all
powerful and dwelling in light unapproachable. He

demands reverence. But He is also willing to be *Father* to such as come to Him by His ordained road, Jesus Christ, and as a Father He tenderly stoops to the immaturity of the babe in Christ. This is the only explanation I have to offer for the following facts. God answered prayers which were unworthy even to have been brought before His presence. If I prayed those same prayers today He would *not* answer them. He responded then, ignoring the selfish vanity of the request, simply because of the honest seeking at the base. He knew I meant it when I said I would give Him my whole life. *The Father seeketh such to worship Him—in spirit and in truth.*

For some three months after my "bargain" I experienced nothing convincing. I read the Gospels and prayed in private, but did not go to church or show any outward interest in religion. Then one day I was invited to a private dance at the home of a girl friend, Jill. Jill had moved away to a different part of town and probably did not know that I had broken with Ben, but as she did not inquire as to whether or not I wanted him to be my partner, I had no opportunity to tell her. She usually gave a dance once a season and invited Ben only because he went with me, her friend. She usually just invited him and left it to him to arrange for my escort to and from her house. So as I prepared to go, I wondered if he would be there.

But on my arrival he wasn't there, and I prepared to enjoy the evening thoroughly, for it was a small home dance with just our crowd, and I loved my friends dearly. Jill's new house was center-halled, so that for dancing we had three spaces—parlor, hall, and dining room. I was dancing with Les (Cora's

friend and long since her dear husband) when it
happened. We had circled out into the hall when the
doorbell rang. Jill opened the door and I beheld Ben,
Reba with him, and he was ushering her into the
house! I could hardly believe my eyes that he would
have dared to do such a thing—it was like slapping
my face publicly. And the dance was so small that
there was no avoiding constant contact. I became
completely unnerved. Trembling from head to foot,
I began to walk all over Les's feet. Long hours of
study, late hours of dancing, unhappy broken sleep
had wrecked my nerves. I was undone—there was
simply no escape from the humiliating fact. Les's
look of respectful compassion did not help my
chagrin. I could not fool Les about the cause of my
agony and the knowledge was too much for my
pride.

"Les, I don't feel well—will you please excuse
me?" I said, and, stopping at the foot of the hall
staircase, I fled up to the bedroom assigned as our
dressing room. Up and down the floor I paced in a
rage at myself, trying to use pride to whip my trembling body into control. It was perfectly useless—I
shook like an aspen leaf.

Suddenly I remembered I was trying to prove if
there was a God. With almost a sneer at such a ridic-
ulous thing, I nevertheless prayed, "O God, if You
are, please give me p—" but I did not have time
to finish the sentence. Something like an electric cur-
rent struck me, shot me through and I tingled all
over. *It had come from above, and from outside
myself.* But it left me completely poised and quiet.
Incredulous, I stretched out my hand—it was steady
and firm. Without stopping to say "Thank You," and
marveling inwardly, I turned and ran down the stairs.

That same dance number was still on and Les was still standing at the foot of the staircase where I had left him.

"I'm all right now, Les," I said gaily. "Let's finish." Which we did. A wonderful exultation, a feeling as if I had new life pulsed through me and continued all evening. Ben asked for a dance and made no effort to conceal his admiration. "You are beautiful tonight," he whispered, but I gave an evasive answer. Our ideals were too different: I must not let my affections get involved again.

The evening was a triumph of gratified pride and vanity for me. But when I was alone in my bedroom, emotional reaction set in. Ben was a superb dancer, and my longing to float through life in perfect rhythm together with him would not be challenged by common sense. Sleep again departed from me and I tossed in agony until morning.

But the one fact stood out. I had cried to God for help, my lips twisted in sardonic unbelief that He even existed, but He had answered swiftly. This was no instance of mind acting upon matter, for the mind had held no faith at all. But help had come *from the outside entirely.* I was now convinced that some Force outside me, intelligent, loving, and powerful, was Up There trying to get in touch with me. Never again did I pray *if Thou art.* And now I wanted to know—how much could I ask of Him? Did He always answer prayer in Jesus' name? Morning and night I now prayed in faith. Those prayers were still all selfish and this is the part of my story where I do not want any young readers to try to imitate me.

Follow me in my pursuit of God—yes.

Like me, come to Him by way of the Christ of Calvary—yes.

Seek for the revelation of that Christ in the Bible
—yes. But don't imitate my flounderings. I was pig-
headed now in the matter of refusing all human advice, and my own level of living was so low that God
could not meet me on a higher one.

I wondered if God could answer seemingly impossible requests: for instance—would He get me invitations to certain balls and dances? It was our senior
year and almost all our "gang" were paired off now,
either engaged or going steady. There was no one
within the circle of my close acquaintances who
would be free to invite me unless I hinted—which I
did not intend to do, ever. God had answered prayer
wonderfully, causing my incredulity to marvel at *His
power* to do it. I will tell of one instance.

A neighboring university had sent their football
team to play ours and a *thé dansant* was to be given
to the two teams after the match. It was purposely
a small affair in honor of the teams, just the players
and their girl friends and such team officers as the
coach and manager. Now Ben was one of the star
players and I wanted to go. He had barged in on my
party, and now I wanted to go to this affair held in
his honor to show that I was not dependent on him
for a good time. Not only was I moved by a thoroughly low and fleshly reason, but also it was hopeless to expect an invitation to such an exclusive
party. Could God do it? I challenged Him.

At last the day before the match arrived. No
one would ask me now—it would be an insult for
any man to ask a girl at such a late hour, sure proof
that she was only second or third choice.

That last afternoon a fellow student and I had
arranged a rehearsal of a theatrical scene in which he
and I were to act alone. George was a good friend

of mine and engaged to a girl called Martha. He also happened to be on the manager's staff of the football team, but this I did not know then. He had come to my house for the rehearsal and after it was over and he reached for his hat to leave, he said, "Well, Isobel, see you at the *thé dansant* tomorrow afternoon after the match." Then I saw he did not know I had broken with Ben.

"No, I don't think you will, George," I said slowly.

He whirled around and shot me a keen look. Then, gentleman that he was, he drew himself up and said with fine courtesy, "Isobel, last night Martha was called out of town unexpectedly. I thought I was going to have to 'go stag' to *thé dansant*. May I have the pleasure of your company? I'll explain to Martha —I'm sure she won't mind."

It was just as simple as that. I was almost intoxicated with the wonder of it, and again the afternoon was a great triumph for me. I had more partners seeking me than there were dances, while Reba was more than once a wallflower. In fact, while dancing with me, Ben had to excuse himself to go and find her a partner!

Now, do I really believe that God was responsible for that? I am sure God gave it to me. Moreover, by piling on the triumphs He taught me a lesson I never forgot. I learned that pride and gratified vanity could never bring me peace or happiness. Underneath the gay triumphant surface I was miserable. My heart was often like lead even while my lips were chattering merry nonsense. This kind of life would never satisfy me. I grew more and more unhappy and disillusioned. And that was what God wanted. It was as if He said, "If this is what you think you want, dear, have some more!" And He stuffed the froth of

life down me. Yet every time He got me an invitation
when humanly speaking it seemed impossible, He
proved to me again that there was nothing He could
not do for me.

All during this time, my parents knew nothing of
my inward seekings. They sensed a change was going
on, but I still refused to go to church with them and
usually spent Sunday trying to catch up on the sleep
I had lost at dances during the week! But there may
have been a softening visible, for Mother began again
to try to help me

"Isobel, I want you to come with me to hear Professor Ellis. The meeting is just a Bible class, not
held in a church, but in a classroom of the Vancouver Bible School. Just to please your mother.
Won't you do a little thing like this to please me?
I don't want to go alone."

And so I went.

I did not know that anyone else in that room knew
me. In fact, I did not look at the audience, for I had
ceased to be interested in human beings. But the
speaker held my attention. Professor Ellis was a cultured, educated Christian gentleman. I liked his
quiet, refined manner of speech. He was speaking
that day on the Temptation of Christ, and as he went
on to give his message, he also very frankly pointed
out the liberal interpretation of that passage. Without
any belligerent dogmatism, he courteously but deftly
refuted their arguments. I saw clearly that here was
a scholar who knew both sides of the argument. Here
was a real gentleman who would never stoop to nasty
remarks about an opponent. And, watching the quiet
radiance of his face, I instinctively knew that here
was a man who had *personal experience with God*

I decided that this was the preacher for me—I would come again.

Seated behind me was another Christian gentleman. White-headed, shy and reserved, he was known to me only as Mr. Wright, a friend of my father's. I forget if it was that first time I went to Professor Ellis' Bible class, or on a succeeding occasion, but at the close of the meeting he leaned forward and spoke to me.

"Isobel, I'm glad to see you here," he said, his eyes flooded with tears. "I've been praying for you for some seven years."

I was stunned. It was about seven years since I had decided to dance and go in for worldly things against my father's pleadings. The yearning in Christ which lit up Mr. Wright's face stirred me to the depths, for my soul still knew periods of agony. With eyes as flooded as his own, I tried to murmur "Thank you," then escaped quickly from the building.

But every Sunday saw me back in that afternoon service, and weekly I was fed and nourished in the truth of God's Word. Professor Ellis' scholarship and his expository preaching combined with his gentle culture had won my full confidence and I was willing to learn from him.

And so, though my head was still befogged by the Mists of The Flats, my feet were once more planted on the High Way, prepared to climb, and my face steadfastly turned Godward.

CHAPTER FOUR

MY YEAR IN ARABIA

On GRADUATING in May, 1922, at twenty years of age, I needed only five months of Normal School to qualify for a teacher's certificate. My ambition was to be a dean of women and teach English in some university, but I was so young and inexperienced in teaching that I first had to accept an elementary grade school assignment. I could have taken an up-country high school appointment, but Mother would not hear of it. She insisted that I teach in a city school, so because of my inexperience I had to accept a position as teacher of the third grade at the Cecil Rhodes School, Vancouver.

In the meantime my family had moved. My father was roentgenologist to Dr. Ernest Hall of Victoria, B.C., and Mother sold our Vancouver home and purchased a chicken ranch just outside Victoria. This ranch was to be for my brother who had been a soldier in World War I and for whom employment must be found. He thought he would like ranch life.

So in February 1923 I found myself a "schoolmarm" in Vancouver and needing to find a boardinghouse. For the first time in my life I would not live at home, but would be on my own, receiving a monthly salary for which I need account to no one.

The idea was distinctly pleasing. But where would I board?

Somehow I ran into the mother of a girl with whom I had gone to elementary school eight years before. They were a Scottish family, and the mother especially was a very superior person. Mrs. McMillan was a thinker, but, inbred with theosophy, had fallen in with the idea that it was wrong to spank a child. I have wondered if this was not the reason her children did more as they liked than as she liked. The two youngest would not continue school, so had to take employment below their family cultural level. By the time I had graduated, Mrs. McMillan was so reduced in circumstances that she was trying to run a boardinghouse and asked if I would come to her. She was apologetic, for she had lost her best furniture and could not provide anything as comfortable as I had been accustomed to, but she was very clean, an excellent cook, and her house was within walking distance of my school. Mother knew her and felt at ease that I should be with Mrs. McMillan, who was as loving and kind to me as if I were her own child.

So I found myself in this house—the only Christian. The two daughters were both engaged to sailors. The youngest child, a son, was a policeman with a wife and small baby. The policeman's brother-in-law, whom we called Laurie, was attending Normal School, hoping to become a schoolteacher. As he was not yet earning, he paid but a minimum rate of board, if anything. This was the household among whom I became the ninth.

After graduation my particular clique scattered. Many went to other universities for further degrees. Some taught school, but went upcountry where they could get high school positions. In no time at all I

seemed to be alone and living in a different world.
The young people of my boardinghouse were very
nice to me, but were all for the gay life. I did not
care to join them. We had little in common but our
boardinghouse. Surrounded with young laughter and
noise, I was as alone as if I had been in the deserts
of Arabia. For a year and a half, God shut me up to
that aloneness, so that I have always called it *my
year in Arabia.*

A young fellow we will call Mac had begun to ask
me out. He was still studying and invited me to the
various big dances of the university from time to
time, but as he did not live in Vancouver our dates
were not frequent.

I had begun to attend evening lectures at the Vancouver Bible School, but it was just beginning and
I do not remember meeting other Christian young
people. I was lonely.

F. B. Meyer points out that this is one of the
planned training schools of God. "One symptom of
being on that path is loneliness." He continues:

> Nothing strengthens us so much as isolation and
> transplantation . . . under the wholesome demand
> his soul will put forth all her native vigor . . . it
> may not be necessary for us to withdraw from
> home and friends; but we shall have to withdraw
> our heart's deepest dependence from all earthly
> props and supports, if ever we are to learn what
> it is to trust simply and absolutely on the eternal
> God.[1]

For one thing I found it hard to keep my prayer
times. The others in the house played cards and
danced or had what they called a good time until
long past midnight. I could not pray with those noises
in my ears. To get up early to pray was not the

---

[1] *Abraham,* by F. B. Meyer.

answer, for once I was up, my mind went rushing on to my schoolteaching, which, by the way, I was finding difficult. At last I hit on the plan of asking the Lord to wake me up at two o'clock in the morning, after the house had settled to quiet, when I would arise for an hour's prayer and Bible study. This worked wonders. Always a sleepyhead, it was wonderful to me to be awakened each morning, as I was, and in the quiet of that still hour Christ became so real to me that often I felt I could have touched Him, if I but put out my hand. I was learning what Dr. A. W. Tozer calls "the awareness of His presence." [2] It satisfied me as nothing on earth had ever done, and filled me with a joy of communion that is inexpressible. It was in this *Arabia* that I learned fellowship with Christ, a living Person-to-person fellowship which henceforth became dearer than anything else in life to me.

The acute sense of His presence was not given during the first few months I was at the McMillan boardinghouse. My head was still in The Misty Flats and my feet were too entangled with the world. How I got lifted out into a clear spiritual atmosphere is a story in itself, so I give it here.

It began with an angry disappointment.

But I must first explain that I was not happy teaching third grade eight-year-olds. The children in my class fascinated me. It was my first real connection with children, for I was the baby of our family and we had early moved away from where small cousins lived. I was totally inexperienced with children and thought them "the cutest things." Even their little buttons of noses fascinated me. Needless to say, I had discipline problems! The little cherubs

[2] *The Pursuit of God*, by A. W. Tozer.

soon found out that their teacher was a softy and
she was given daily samples of what unexpectedly
naughty things a cherub can think up—even without
ever losing his angelic smile!

Then the subjects I taught were so elementary—
spelling, arithmetic tables, simple nature studies and
physical drill. Eight hours each day one's delightful
mental life must be tied down to such boredom. I
have often thought that if I had been allowed to
teach high school English I might never have become
a missionary—I would have loved it.

But now I hated teaching. I found the discipline so
perplexing that I was afraid I was going to be a failure and became thoroughly alarmed. This was to
be my life-work! I decided I must study teaching and
so signed up for a Teachers' Convention in Seattle
during—was it Easter holidays? I've forgotten.

Now, in Seattle there was a boy-friend who had
corresponded with me since grade school, which we
had attended together—the General Wolfe School in
South Vancouver. I had not seen Donald for years,
but when I wrote that I was coming to the Convention I got a letter right back saying I must stay at his
house and he would be at the boat to meet me. So
it was arranged.

I was just about to leave for the Seattle boat when
a telegram was handed me. It read: HAVE ARRANGED
FOR YOU TO STAY AT WHIPPLES SEATTLE LOVE
DADDY.

Was I annoyed! "Daddy, how perfectly mean of
you," I muttered to myself. "Oh, when will you and
Mother stop interfering with my plans and realize
that I am grown up?" The Whipples—who are they?
Dim memory finally produced vague outlines. "Oh,
religious friends of Dad's. Yes, I remember now. So

that's Dad's idea. Wants to have them talk to me
about my soul, eh? Well, they won't find a porcupine
more receptive. I'm just *not* going to be bossed like
this. I'll wire them that I've made other plans." But
a glance at the clock showed me I had no time to
send a telegram if I were to catch the ship. Thoroughly provoked I went aboard to my cabin. By
morning we would be in Seattle.

Don was there all right and I explained my predicament. He was not put out. "Well, just sleep
there," he suggested. "I can take you around from
there." And so it was decided.

I don't remember anything of the Convention. I
remember a nice supper with Don afterward, and
an evening of fun—a dance perhaps. Anyway, I did
not realize how late the hour was until we approached the Whipple house and found it in darkness. No—there was a dim light at the back. The
door-bell ring produced other lights, then the door
was opened by Mrs. Otis Whipple herself. Don was
introduced and invited in, but he declined and said
good-by—and I found myself in the sitting room
alone with my hostess.

I do not know the kind of person I was looking
for, but it certainly was not the kind I met. Motherly
plumpness, a cheery voice, Southern warmth of hospitality, geniality and culture were what greeted me.
Culture is a form of beauty, the beauty of a trained
mind and heart trained to think of the other person's
feelings. Beauty of any kind has always had power
over me and I was drawn to her immediately. Instinctively I knew she was not one to barge into my
inner sanctum without an invitation. As yet I did
not know that there are other ways of soul-winning!

God and my soul were never mentioned—just a

charming talk about my home, their old friendship with my father, of a girl, Tony Black, to whom I was supposed to bear striking likeness. She spoke of a summer conference at a place called The Firs, and of her husband's sister, a missionary in China recently widowed who was to be at The Firs this summer of 1923. More and more I relaxed; better and better I liked her. So finally when I was shown to my room my porcupine quills were all safely laid flat.

The next day was Sunday. I had resolved to bend to decorum enough to go to church in the morning, then I meant to claim the rest of the day to do what I liked. I had a friend named Mamie in the city, and had an appointment to spend the afternoon with her. Idly I wondered that Mrs. Whipple had not as yet made any effort to get me alone and talk religiously. Little did I dream the truth, which she told me only years later. That first night, after we had all gone to bed, she could not sleep for the burden of *me*. At last she got up and fell to her knees, asking God the cause. For more than an hour she battled in prayer that whatever was the reason He had sent me to them, it might be fulfilled before I left. Not before she felt she had prayed *through* did she go back to bed. Having committed the matter to the Lord, she did not get anxious as to how He would accomplish it. *She did not try to rush matters,* which in my case would have been the end of her possibly influencing me. One of her favorite sayings was, "Flexible in the hands of the Spirit," and she truly lived it.

The afternoon visit to Mamie was very pleasant (I had always loved her) until she asked me an unsettling question: "Isobel, do you like schoolteaching? Are you enjoying your work?"

"Oh, Mamie," I groaned in reply, "I'm not happy at all. All my life I've planned to teach, and now that I've graduated and am at it, I feel like a misfit. And yes, I just hate it. If only I had a high school position, I'm sure it would be different. I'm still sure I would enjoy teaching literature. But I'm only twenty-one, you know, and so could not expect to get right into a city high school without any teaching experience. It's so inane teaching spelling and arithmetic. I just don't——"

"Isobel, I know what you need," struck in Mamie earnestly. "You need to see a phrenologist, and have your head read! He'd tell you what you are fitted for. And it just so happens that a very excellent phrenologist is in town, Dr. X——. He is a friend of ours and coming to supper with us tonight. His charges are very high, but as a friend of ours I'm sure he would do you for nothing. But you would have to come tonight, because he is leaving to-morrow."

"Oh, Mamie," I cried, "how perfectly wonderful! There is only one snag. I'm staying with religious people, and they might be offended at a guest in their house going to see a phrenologist on *Sunday*. You know how particular some people are about keeping the Sabbath. Oh, if they will only consent! My hostess is really a dear and I just couldn't offend her. But I tell you—I'll go right back and ask her. If she says yes, I'll phone you and you make the appointment for me. Oh, it would be grand to be happy in one's work! It would be wonderful to know what one was fitted for in life."

"Well, Dr. X—— will know, I'm sure of that. All right. Good-by. I'll be looking for that phone call!" And we parted, I to return to the Whipples' home with beating heart. Was I about to lose the opportunity of my life because of old-fashioned religious scruples?

Arriving back earlier than expected, I met Mrs. Whipple in the hall, and went straight to the point: "Mrs. Whipple, I would like to ask you a question. Would you object to my going to a phrenologist tonight to have my head read? I've not been very happy in my work and——"

"Well now, dear," she said in her cheery, comfortable way, "let us go upstairs and discuss it. I'm not quite sure I understand all that is involved. Here is Miss McCausland"—waylaying another guest who was crossing the hall at that moment. "Miss McCausland is a schoolteacher herself, and maybe she can help us. Take her to the little front bedroom, Margaret. I'll be there in a moment."

I did not learn until many years later why she delayed in coming. But she ran for prayer help. Her young high school daughter, Lois, was in the back of the house with two friends, all of them in their teens. It is interesting now to look back at those three little maidens who were urged on to their knees downstairs to intercede for the right direction of phrenologist-seeker me upstairs. Lois later became Mrs. Nathan Walton of the China Inland Mission.* Evelyn Watson became her sister-in-law, Mrs. Elden Whipple, while the third young girl, Doris Coffin, became Mrs. Willard Aldrich, author of the well-known column in *Moody Monthly,* "Out of the Mixing Bowl." But at this moment the three teenagers were only told, "Isobel has come to a crisis in her life! Pray her through while I go upstairs and deal with her." So down on their knees they went in prayer.

* Since 1965, Overseas Missionary Fellowship has been the official name.

Upstairs Mrs. Whipple was saying to me, "Now, dear, tell us everything from the beginning so we will understand."

So the flood-gates were unlocked and out poured the story of my schoolteaching troubles and disappointments. I spoke freely because I felt an atmosphere of loving sympathy, and sensed a poise about those two women which seemed to say that *their* lives were satisfying. So I unfolded this wonderful opportunity of having my head read by a skilled phrenologist, and the supposed snag—it was Sunday. With beating heart, I looked up into that kind, wise, and lovely face and said, "Would you object to my going on Sunday?" No tremor of horror or shock crossed her face at all, but she had a look of deep thoughtfulness as if she were weighing the matter carefully.

Then came her answer: "Isobel dear, I don't think the matter of its being Sunday is the important thing. It's like this: *God has a plan for your life*. The Bible says that He has created us unto good works and *foreordained* that we should walk in them (Eph. 2:10). That means He has foreordained a useful life for you, and He does so for each of His creatures. The point as I see it, is to find out God's plan for your life and then follow it. If it is His will to reveal that plan through a phrenologist, going on Sunday would do no harm. But if it were not His will to reveal His plan through a phrenologist, *going any day of the week would be wrong*."

I was struck with the common sense and logic of her words and thrilled through and through to hear that God had a plan for my life. Daughter of an elder in the church and granddaughter of a Presbyterian minister, I do not remember anyone ever tell-

ing me that before. I had always thought that God
was a kindly, fatherly Being. Away off in the heavens
somewhere we could call upon Him in trouble, but
for the rest of the time it was up to us to map out
our own lives in good, honest work. Then we could
ask His blessing and help from time to time. But
that God was so minutely interested in *me,* that He
would take the trouble to plan a career for me—plan
it without my asking—the tender intimacy of a Love
which could do that touched me to the breaking
point. Hardly able to control my voice, I asked,
"Well, how are we to find out His plan for us?"

By this time I was kneeling at the bed on which
Miss McCausland sat, Mrs. Whipple in a chair beside me. She reached for her Bible and opened it
in front of me saying, "Isobel, I've always found His
will *through His Word,* this Book. His plan for us
will always be in accordance with the Scriptures.
And with me, it is usually from the Bible itself that
I get my leading." At that moment the telephone
rang and Mrs. Whipple was called.

"Excuse me a moment, I'll be right back," she
said. "Miss McCausland, will you tell Isobel what
you think?" I do not remember what dear Miss Mc-
Causland said for I was thinking, *God's plan for my
life is in that Book.* Impulsively, I pulled it toward
me. It fell shut and I reopened it at random with
my eyes on Miss McCausland. Inwardly I was wondering what the Bible had to say about phrenology,
when my eye happened to fall on the open page and
there, unconsciously, my left hand lay with the fore-
finger pointing at a verse. I read: "KEEP THEE FAR
FROM A FALSE MATTER" (Ex. 23:7).

It was as if a Voice had spoken to me and I was
so startled at the directness of the answer to my in-

ward question which no one had heard that my distressed heart collapsed with relief. I was weeping when Mrs. Whipple reentered the room—weeping terribly, simply rent with sobs.

"It is all right, Isobel," she tried to say. "He'll lead you."

"Oh, He has," I cried. "Look at this verse!" and I pointed to *Keep thee far from a false matter*. She too marveled at such a quick, thoroughly complete answer. But the piled-up heartaches of a whole year and a half of SEARCHING after God had reached a climax, and I could only sob until exhausted. Very tenderly and lovingly the two ladies ministered to me. Dear Mrs. Whipple never tried to pry: the privacy of the human soul was respected by her, and that was another reason we all loved and trusted her so.

I do not remember anything more of that visit, except that Mrs. Whipple told me again of The Firs Bible Conference and urged me to attend that July as her guest. I was not interested. I still shrank from evangelistic meetings with their worked-up emotion and high pressure methods. I did not intend to be high pressured into anything.

"Thank you, Mrs. Whipple," I said, "but I have already signed up to attend Teachers' Summer School in Victoria. Until God leads differently, I must earn my living and can only do it by teaching." And so we parted.

The Lord now wished to direct my thoughts into a channel where they would never have run of themselves. My life was about to turn a new corner, and strange to say, it all hinged, at first, upon a pair of shoes. But that is the subject of the next chapter.

CHAPTER FIVE

A PAIR OF SHOES AND THE FIRS CONFERENCE

Here, Julia," said Mrs. Tom Cole to her sister-in-law, Mrs. Otis Whipple. "The Firs Conference will soon open and you need a pair of shoes"—with a significant look at her—and she held out a five-dollar bill. I do not know if those were her exact words, but the gift was given for shoes and a significant look along with it, as Mrs. Cole told me herself years later.

Julia Whipple was not one to neglect her personal appearance. To be well groomed had been her life-long habit, but of late funds had not been too plentiful. The story of how Julia and Otis Whipple gave their last earthly possession to the Lord—this honeymoon cabin at The Firs, Bellingham, Washington—and of how God used it to establish the annual Lake Whatcom Bible and Missionary Conference which has been so blessed to themselves, has been told by Doris Coffin Aldrich in a book called *The Firs of the Lord*. Suffice it to say that 1923 was to be only their third attempt at a conference, and Julia Whipple was to be hostess. What would people think of her shabby shoes?

But she had something else on her mind.

She had been praying that Isobel Miller would come to The Firs Conference. She saw, as I had not, that here was one groping blindly toward God, and open to dangerous misleadings if she were not carefully grounded in the Word. As is a young person's weakness, I might be carried off my feet by some magnetic personality of one of the many "isms," if I chanced to meet such, at this stage. I needed grounding in the Scriptures and I needed Christian fellowship. I had a small college debt to pay and had been earning a salary for only six months—maybe money would be a factor in bringing me. At any rate, she waved the matter of new shoes aside, sat down, and wrote a letter urging me to come, saying that the enclosed five dollars, she felt, was the Lord's provision for my boat tickets. Once I reached The Firs I was to be her guest—room and board would cost me nothing. Wouldn't I come?

I received her gift and invitation quite casually, not at all moved with any desire to go. It was Mrs. Whipple's kind heart, I told myself, and now I was forced to do something about it. But I felt my excuse would be an easy one to make. The conference came right in the middle of the summer school I had signed up for. I must get credit for this summer's study, and they would hardly give me full credit for six weeks' work if I ran off in the middle for ten or eleven days! So I made this my test, *and I prayed about it:* "Lord, if it be Thy will for me to go, please move the authorities to grant consent without reducing my credits, and I'll take it as Thy will I am to go."

The next morning found me before the registrar of the Teachers' Summer Institute.

"I have been called to Bellingham on a matter important to me and would like to apply for ten days' absence without reducing my credits. Could that be done, sir?" I asked.

He inquired my name, turned over the pages of a book, pursed his lips a moment, then said, "All right, Miss Miller. Just tell us when you leave and when you will return."

I could not believe my ears. Only the day before a fellow student-teacher had applied for a week off and had been flatly refused! I still do not know how to explain it, but my full credits were given to me.

I came out of the office walking as if in a dream. I inquired about the boat schedule and sent word to Mrs. Whipple that I was coming, how and when, and went home to pack my suitcase.

So it came about that one evening in July, 1923, my boat arrived at the Bellingham pier. I had never been there before and knew no one, but as I looked eagerly around for Mrs. Whipple, a young man and a sweet-faced girl stepped up to me.

"Isobel Miller? We've come to meet you. Elden Whipple and Evelyn Watson—do you remember meeting us in Seattle? We have a car here. Hop in! We have to drive to the conference grounds, but it is not too far."

Their warm friendliness made me feel at home immediately and soon we were whirling out over curving roads with fragrant woods on either hand. It was a twisting labyrinth to me, but finally we turned into a path, drew up among tall fir trees, and there was dear Mrs. Whipple coming to meet me. Her radiance, rippling laugh of joy, and overflowing hospitality was something to cuddle down into. I was duly hugged and kissed, then shown into a big firelit room. Older people sat on chairs, and the younger ones on the floor before the big, crackling open fireplace of logs. The flames threw a golden light over all faces, and the young people pulled me down on the floor to sit with them while the evening devotional service continued. Though always shy and reticent with strangers, here I was soon at home and filled with a wonderful content. The atmosphere was charged with the presence of the One whom I was learning to know and adore, and He was the center of everyone else's attention too.

In the doorway I had been introduced to "my sister-in-law, Mrs. Edna Whipple Gish, whose story I told you in Seattle. She is to be your cabin mate." Years afterward I asked Mrs. Whipple if this had been a premeditated arrangement, for it was to have a lasting effect on my life.

"I can't remember that it was," she said simply. "Edna's was the only cabin with a spare space, as I remember it."

After the campfire service Edna led me through a woodsy path to the little cabin in the woods where she and I were to live. We slept together, but before going to sleep she pulled out a little worn Bible from beneath her pillow and read a chapter with me, prayed, then at "lights out" we settled down with the perfume of the fir trees soothing us into slumber.

I had time to think back over Edna's story just before falling asleep.

"This is Ellis's Bible," she had said to me as she reverently took the worn, much-marked book from beneath the pillow. Then I remembered what Mrs. Whipple had told me in Seattle.

Edna had met Ellis when he was on his first furlough, and found him her ideal. He was a young man of deep devotion and consecration, and together they had gone to China to the South Gate section of Nanking.

The next year they went for their vacation to beautiful Kuling, a famous mountain resort, where there is a pool and good swimming, also many lovely walks.

One morning they had decided on a swim—both were expert swimmers. As they left their tent they heard a cry from the pool. Ellis immediately ran and dived in to the rescue—a young missionary had caught a cramp and had gone down. Ellis was successful and saved her life, but he himself disappeared. Then Edna dived in to search for him. As time dragged on and she could not find him, one can imagine the terror and anguish of her feelings. Diving, searching, she did not notice that her body was being bruised and battered against the rocks. *Ellis*— that was all she thought of. Finally she saw his body washed up behind a little waterfall. Again she dived, reached him, dragged his body with her and got it to shore. But life had gone.

Exhausted, she sank on a tree stump and covered her face with her hands.

A few minutes later she happened to look up and saw some Chinese coolies standing terrified with the dead man before them. Quickly she approached them and explained that the body on the ground was not her husband—that he was safe with God—and she preached Christ to them.

Edna herself was so bruised that she was sent to the hospital and later advised to take a short furlough. Ellis's insurance money was enough to bring her to The Firs for the summer, and the conference council had asked her to lead the young people's meetings. We never knew what it was costing her to set aside her daily heartbreak and be our cheery, radiant Bible teacher. Years later Mrs. Whipple told me how Edna would go to the council and tell them she could not continue, but they would promise to pray for her, and back she would come to us.

She laid before us the Scriptural challenge to a consecrated life and to missionary service. I had never given the foreign field one thought up to that time. I was a stay-at-home body by disposition and a veritable slave to physical comforts. Travel never attracted me, for it meant strange faces and strange ways—in other words, discomfort. Edna was the first to show me that I ought to be willing to give this up, if God asked me to do so. When finally she gave a challenge to those who would surrender for foreign service, if He called, I put up my hand. I was surprised to see how thrilled she was. For to me it was a matter of course. That night I had made my bargain with God: I had promised Him my life. If He wanted it on the foreign field—why, of course, then I must go to the foreign field. It was not a question of if I wanted to go or not—*I was no longer my own*. At the time I had no clear indication that it *was* the foreign field He wanted. I was willing, if it were, to go—that was all. Why were they all so excited that I had raised my hand?

A much deeper blessing Edna had unwittingly brought me. Cabin life with her was my first encounter with a Spirit-filled life living in its daily routine habits. It was Edna *off the platform* who wrought most for me.

She sought the Lord's face before that of anyone else at the beginning of each day. There was no wake-up chatter and pillow-flinging nonsense at dawn. This deeply bruised heart hungered and panted after the Lord, and her first waking thought was a longing for His fellowship and presence. And she kindled the same hunger in me. Remember, I had a bruised heart, too.

She read Philippians with me and Ellis's marginal notes.

"This one thing I do"—how it smote home, because this precept was lived out before my eyes. I marked it in my Bible, too.

"Rejoice always"—Edna had attained to that. How could I ever learn the secret? I marked the verse, but decided to try for Philippians 4:11 as perhaps more within the possibility of attainment: "For I have learned, in whatsoever state I am, therewith to be content." This became my life-verse for the next ten years or so.

"That I may know him, and the power of his resurrection, and the fellowship of his sufferings, being made conformable unto his death" (Phil. 3:10). Great words that moved me to the depths of my being—I was on that quest. But little did I know, beyond that mere fact, that my feet were on the High Way—I was searching for Him.

CHAPTER SIX

EXTINGUISHED TAPERS

Who extinguishes their taper
 Till they hail the rising sun?
Who discards the garb of winter
 Till the summer has begun?
            —Anonymous

IT WILL DOUBTLESS ASTONISH some adult readers
and perhaps make them shake their heads dubiously
to learn that all this time I was still indulging in
theaters, dances, and other worldly things. My father
had long years before urged me to separate myself
from these amusements, but my mother felt he was
narrow in his views on such matters, and that they
did no harm if indulged in discriminately. So I had
gone along with her viewpoint as the easier and more
pleasant.

Occasionally I had wondered about it, but had
always been sharply conscious of that old taunt,
"You do this, or believe this, because your papa told
you so." I was not going to give up any habit just
because some human being told me to! If *God* told
me to stop them I would obey. Otherwise I would
continue as I had been.

These amusements were like the *taper* of our verse.
They formed the light moments of my life, and I

wasn't going to give up any *fun* just because some old religious fogey was prejudiced against it!

The first taper that I extinguished was card-playing. In McMillan's boardinghouse the young folk often played until past midnight, and if they had the wherewithal they put up some small stakes. I suppose the sailors thought a game inane if it did not have the element of gain or loss to stimulate them. Of course, they called me in to play with them. I hesitated—more from reluctance to waste time and my precious pennies than for any other reason.

"Maybe Isobel doesn't think she should play cards, because she is religious," offered Jack gravely. Jack was one of the sailors, but very open to counsel. He even asked me to teach him the Bible at one time, and I believe he would have accepted the Lord if his wife and the others had not pulled him away. I grabbed at this offer of a legitimate excuse in order to get out of such invitations easily.

"Well, to tell the truth, Jack, I would prefer not to," I answered.

"Then we're not going to tease her into it," Jack informed everybody. "You play the piano for us, Isobel! We'd like some music while we play cards."

I loved to play the piano and preferred hymns above everything else. Those young people did not object to my religious selections, so the strange anomaly took place night after night. They played cards and gambled while I played from my hymn-book. Of course, this left me free to go to bed as early as I liked and the arrangement pleased me well. But having given up card-playing, supposedly for religious reasons, I must in consistency hold to it on other occasions. So I did just that. It cost me nothing. I always thought cards were a tiresome waste of good mental energy—they achieved nothing but amusement, and I did not find them very amusing. So out went the taper of card-playing.

It was during the summer of 1923, perhaps before I went to The Firs, that I had to extinguish a second taper. This was quite a different affair and one concerning which no human being had ever spoken to me.

I was a voracious reader of romantic fiction. Novels gripped me and were my favorite mental escape from trials and difficulties, or from an evening which had to be spent alone. With a good love story I was immediately transported into another world, and if the plot was exciting I could not put the book down until I finished it.

We were living with my brother on his ranch for the summer, and as there were no other young people around I had to occupy many evenings and found a good novel was my first resort. This particular time, it was an exciting story that I could not lay down. I never did read the modern sexy novels, but chose clean, exciting love stories. Very often these were not really true to life. Life does contain moments of adventure, but these times are interspersed with long periods of plain, unvarnished hard work. The real things of life are attained at these monotonous level periods, so to speak, more than they are at the high peaks of excitement. People who in their reading feed on the lurid and melodramatic are not prepared for the long stretches of routine work which fill every life. I believe this is partly responsible for many broken marriages today. Young people think married life should be all moonlight and thrills, and they balk when they find themselves on the level stretches of plain, ordinary working together, which actually are the real life and backbone of a home.

Anyway, I was deep in the excitement of the book. Midnight came and I was so near the end that I could not stop. In fact, it was one o'clock in the morning before I finished the book and took up my Bible for evening devotions. But I got no blessing from it. Never had the Bible seemed so drab and dull. When I tried to pray, the Lord seemed far away. *It's just sleepiness,* I told myself, and curled up for slumber.

But the next morning things were little better. God still seemed far away and the Bible stuffy and uninteresting. Before the Teachers' Summer Institute opened I was clerking in a Bible Depot which belonged to my father. He had felt that Victoria lacked a Christian bookstore so, supported by Christian friends, he had opened this Bible Depot as a sideline. I substituted for the clerk while she was on summer vacation, and traveling into town by bus gave me time to think. What had happened to me, that the Lord seemed no longer real? And why had the Bible, which I had begun to read through from Genesis to Revelation for the first time in my life— why had the Bible become insipid? I was alarmed. Sitting in the bus, I talked to the Lord about it in my heart.

"Oh Lord, what is wrong with me?" I prayed. "Why can't I sense Your Presence now as I have lately? Why has the Bible become dry?"

"When a child fills her stomach with ice cream and soda pop," the Lord seemed to answer, "why does she lose her appetite for meat and potatoes?"

"Lord, do You mean the novel did that to me?"

"It excited all the fleshly part of your nature,

didn't it? Did it do *anything* to help you spiritually?"

"Nothing, Lord. It kept me up so late. I'm tired this morning. Lord, if I promise to give up novel reading, will You come back to me? Will the Bible come alive to me again?"

"Try it and see."

From that moment, the Lord was real and present once more and the Word took on new meaning. My spiritual growth could have been traced by the markings in that Bible as I read it from cover to cover. I discovered verses that seemed to spring out of the page as His voice to meet my need at the moment. One verse I remember particularly: "For the mountains shall depart and the hills be removed; but my kindness shall not depart from thee, neither shall the covenant of my peace be removed, saith the Lord that hath mercy on thee" (Isa. 54:10). I have claimed this verse through the years and it has been fulfilled to me.

I hardly need say that the taper of novel reading, which included magazine stories, was extinguished from that day on. For about fifteen years I never permitted myself to read a love story. After that, when I had to be alone in Lisuland so often, with problems pressing upon me, I used to read a bit at mealtimes, usually the old classics of Dickens, Thackeray, Brontë, and Barrie. These I had read before so they had no hold on me to continue reading past mealtime, and they did give me a wholesome mental holiday for an hour, lifting me out of the canyon-world back into life among my own race.

Did I find it hard to make this self-denial? Does one miss candlelight when morning sunshine is pouring in the window? No, I was richly repaid for this self-discipline.

The next taper that the Lord touched was my dancing. Mac continued to invite me to the university big dances, and to some of the smaller ones occasionally. It was at one of the latter—probably a fraternity dance—that I ran into Marion A—— in the dressing room. Marion was a Christian girl in our year who had abstained all through her course from worldly amusements. We had both graduated now and here we met *at a dance!*

"Why, Marion!" I exclaimed in surprise.

"Well, you are to blame, Isobel Miller," she said with her merry frankness. "You are the reason I am here tonight. You are a Christian too, aren't you? And all through our four years you danced and had a good time while I got left out of everything. People say you are a good Christian, but you dance, so I decided to dance, too. This is my first dance."

I did not know it at the moment, but this was my last dance. I do not know how Marion ended up, but I fear she drifted from the Lord.

For one memorable dance I had as partner a science major named Keith whom I had known since high school days. As we were waltzing around he made some contemptuous remark about "old-fashioned fogies who believe in God." *Ah,* said I to myself, *here is my chance to witness.* I always felt that if I kept in touch with the dancing crowd, it would afford me contacts for Christ with people who would not be contacted otherwise. So I started in eagerly, "Keith, why do you say that? I believe in God, and you used to."

"Oh, that was before I met Dr. Sedgewick or studied science," he replied impatiently. "No one with a scientific approach to life believes that old stuff any more."

"Oh, but they do!" I cried eagerly. "I have been investigating God and have indubitable proof that He exists!"

"What proof?" he scoffed. Then I tried to tell him, but he refused to believe. He got angry and we were arguing together hotly when a ripple of laughter brought us to ourselves. The orchestra had stopped playing, the dancers had taken their seats. Only Keith and I were left on the floor. Unconscious that the number had ended, we were waltzing round and round in the center of the room obviously fighting over something.

"Better give up, Keith!" called out a pal from the sidelines. "A woman convinced against her will is of the same opinion still. They never give in and they don't know how to reason!"

When Keith saw what a laughingstock we had made of ourselves he swore angrily, marched me to a seat and stalked off in high dudgeon. If there is one thing a man can't forgive, it is a wound to his pride. I had caused Keith a public humiliation and he cut me dead from that hour. My testimony to him had not only been a failure, it had left him more antagonistic than ever.

It was a very subdued and thoughtful Isobel whom Mac saw home that night. Was this the Lord speaking to me? I had led Marion A—— astray. I had further antagonized Keith. Was dancing worth all this?

A few nights later Mac telephoned to me and asked me to the Agricultural Ball—in April, I think it was to be. "Mac, I'm not sure," I parried. "That is so far ahead. Call me a little later, will you?" I would need to pray about it before going to another dance. Was this only an accident or was the Lord speaking to me about giving up this amusement?

I was in the throes of indecision when the telephone rang again and a cherry voice with a rippling laugh called me from the other end. "Guess who is speaking, Isobel!" Only one person had such a contagious, delightful approach.

"Mrs. Whipple!" I cried in joy, almost trying to jump into the receiver. 'Are you in town? Can I get to see you?"

"That you may," was the answer. "We are here on some business for a day or two and staying with Mrs. Ernest Walsh. Can you come out, or shall we come to you?"

McMillan's boardinghouse was no place for a quiet discussion. "Oh, I'll come to you," I cried. "Tell me how to get there." Inside of an hour I was in the parlor of Mrs. Walsh's home, seated on a stool at Mrs. Whipple's feet. Oh, it was the most wonderful feeling just to be near her again! Mr. Whipple was one with her, but had a shy silent disposition which took time and experience to appreciate. She often appealed to him for his opinion, however, and it was always worth waiting for.

"Well, tell me what you have been doing since the conference," she said gaily.

"That is just what I want to do," I answered, "for I have a pressing problem. Just before you called, a boy friend phoned to ask me to the Aggie dance and I put him off but told him I'd tell him definitely a little later. I'm all in a stew about it." Then I told her of my adventure with Keith. Mrs. Whipple probably was scandalized to see that the girl she thought had been led into full consecration was still deep in worldly amusements, *but she didn't show it.* To have looked shocked at my doings would have made me resentful—for wasn't I *honestly* seeking the Lord and His will? I was merely refusing to act on *Your papa and your mama told you so.*

Mrs. Whipple gave a significant glance at her husband, then answered me sweetly: "I can quite see that you are in a mess, Isobel. You are trying to serve two masters at one time, and it always has painful results. Let's see what the Word of God says." She opened her Bible to I Corinthians 6:12 and read: " 'All things are lawful unto me, but all things are not expedient.' You are compromising, Isobel, and that is fatal whatever realm it occurs in. Have you ever told Mac that you have become a Christian?"

"Oh, no," answered this product of the twentieth century. "Our set doesn't do that. It is a point of honor among us not to thrust our religious opinions upon the other fellow. I've never told anyone! It is my private life with God."

Poor Mrs. Whipple! What a warped little human being she had to deal with! But she was full of faith and of the Holy Ghost.

"Those are standards of your old life, Isobel," she said gently. "II Corinthians 5:17 says that 'if any man be in Christ, he is a new creature: *old things are passed away;* behold all things are become new.' "

What a lovely verse! It sounded as if it had been written just for me. Then and there I marked it in my Bible.

"But look at II Corinthians 6:14-17, Isobel," went on my dear spiritual mother. " 'Be ye not unequally yoked together with unbelievers. . . . What communion hath light with darkness? . . . Wherefore

come out from among them and be ye separate, saith
the Lord.' That is the basis of our separation from
things of the world and standards of the world.
I Peter 3:15 says that we should be ready always to
give a reason of the hope that is in you. I think it
is your duty, under the standards of your new life
with God, to tell your friends about Christ and what
He has done for you. You will be surprised at the
spiritual blessing it will bring."

"But I did try to tell Keith," I wailed, simply terrified at this idea of witnessing.

"But look at the place you were in when you told
him," went on Mrs. Whipple. "You stood in the
place of compromise and worldliness and then expected him to respect your testimony. No wonder he
despised it. But now if you take your stand against
dancing as belonging to your old life and unsuitable
to the new, I believe you will find Mac showing a
different reaction."

"Well, I'll try," I said dully. Young people always
think that the older folk don't understand their generation. Inwardly I felt this way at the moment and
dreaded speaking plainly to Mac. He had been so
kind to me. I shrank from offending him or rendering myself odious in his eyes as I had done to Keith.

All the next day I dreaded that evening phone call,
and when the moment came I went cold all over and
was nearly paralyzed with fright. But I gritted my
teeth and took up the receiver. It was Mac, all right.

"Well, Isobel," he said, "what is the decision about
the Aggie ball?"

My throat was so dry I could hardly get the words
out.

"Mac," I answered, "I hope you will forgive me.
But I have become a Christian lately and have de-

cided to give up dancing altogether. I do not criticize the gang in this matter, but I have had some experiences which make me feel that God would not have me continue to dance. I'm sorry not to have told you before—I was just undecided."

There was a long silence at the other end, during which my heart beat so violently I was afraid he could hear it. I was trembling from head to foot.

At length Mac's voice came over the wire: "Thank you, Isobel, for being so straightforward with me. I honor you for not playing with me about this. May I have the pleasure of your company to the baccalaureate service on Sunday instead?"

"Oh, thank you, Mac!" I said. "Yes, indeed. I would be delighted to go with you."

"It's a date, then. I'll call for you at nine-thirty. Good-by."

I staggered to my room and fell across my bed in the weakness of relief. Mrs. Whipple had been right after all. Mac had said he *honored* me for being straightforward! And to prove it he had asked for another date immediately! Oh, how good of the Lord to let it happen that way. How did Mrs. Whipple know? She knew the general principles of life—that compromise wins respect from no one, but a straightforward testimony does. Clean-cut action does, too. The older generation may not understand all the new scientific terms of the young generation, but they know the principles of life which never change. And it is a wise youngster who will not discard the inheritance of wisdom and experience from those who have gone before.

So the taper of dancing was extinguished, and forgotten very quickly as the Rising Sun flooded my life with new and fascinating interests.

There remained but one taper now, the theater. I had gone only to good movies, an occasional classic opera, or wholesome family theater acts. There could be no harm in such, I thought, and they taught one much of human nature.

The last one I went to was a sweet, harmless story —I think it was *Smilin' Thro'*. I enjoyed it very much, but as I went home, once more all the old longings for romance and storybook experiences flooded me. The music, too, had stirred up the emotional side of me and once more prayer was a blank and the Bible had lost its savor. In vain I tried to push through to the Lord's presence. "My Beloved had withdrawn Himself and was gone" was as true of me as of the little bride in the Song of Solomon. "I sought Him but I could not find Him: I called Him, but He gave me no answer." Later, when I read the Song of Solomon and came to this incident, I knew what it meant, perfectly. I had been there myself—this, for the second time.

"Oh, Lord," I prayed, "if You will but return to me I will never go to the theater again. You may have that also."

"It was but a little that . . . I found him whom my soul loveth: I held him and would not let him go" (S.S. 3:4).

Nothing was worth the loss of fellowship with Him. Then did the Sun of Righteousness arise in my heart with healing in His wings.

I remember only once being tempted to relight this last taper. Remember how alone I was, how young, how accustomed to having many friends of my own age. It was an evening, perhaps in May, when everything in youth was calling for companionship and fun. The McMillan young folk were all going out together to see a movie and I would be left alone in the house.

"Oh, come on, Isobel," they teased, catching me by the hand. "It's a good clean movie tonight—can't possibly do you any harm. What does a young girl like you want to mope in the house for on such a lovely evening? Be companionable—come on with us!" They were a kindhearted group and I was sorely tempted to go. The perfumed May air called to me from the open doorway. I was about to yield when I saw a doubtful look in Jack's eyes.

"Don't press her to do what she doesn't feel is right," he said quietly. That settled it.

"No, thank you," I returned. "Have a good time!" and waved them gaily off, then turned to go upstairs with a heavy heart. I entered my room, drab, rather dark, with its cheap furniture, and cried into the silence of the empty house, "Oh, Lord, is it to be so dull always? And I'm still young! A girl looks her nicest at twenty-one or two. Nobody to go with! Nothing to do but Bible study! Oh Lord, speak to me!" And I pulled over my Bible and opened it at random.

The words on the page sprang up before me: "Then said Jesus unto the twelve, Will ye also go away? Then Simon Peter answered him, Lord, to whom shall we go? thou hast the words of eternal life" (John 6:67-68).

I sat there reading and re-reading that quiet, potent question. God did not refuse to let me go back to my earthly tapers. He just wanted me to think well before I did. Did I really prefer them? Would I change places with any one of the three girls who had just left the house? God forbid—I shrank from such a thought. Did I want to go back to Ben's world of loose loyalties? Again I shuddered. *Lord, to whom shall we go?* There was no other road. The low road? Not for a moment. The Misty Flats? God deliver me from ever again drifting around there! Then there remained only The High Way.

"Forgive me, Lord," I bowed my head in contrition. "There is no one I want but Thee. Please comfort me." Then the sense of His Presence so filled the room that it is too sacred to talk about. Suffice it to say, that I never again looked back, but more and more learned the value of communion alone with Himself.

Dr. Tozer has pointed out how our generation is in danger of missing this sacred joy. He says: "We have been trying to apply machine-age methods to our relations with God . . . our thought habits are those of the scientist, not those of the worshiper. We are more likely to explain than to adore." *Searching* is a scientific procedure, but we want to beware that it does not get into mechanical ruts. "We read our chapter, have our short devotions, and rush away, hoping to make up for our deep inward bankruptcy by attending another Gospel meeting, or listening to another thrilling story told by a religious adventurer lately returned from afar."

We need to worship and to adore as well as to analyze and explain. Mary of Bethany learned much by just sitting at Jesus' feet, listening to Him and loving Him. Our generation's greatest lack is just here.

By the summer of 1924, unknown to me, my year in Arabia was over. Mac had gone out of the city on a summer job. When he returned I was in Chicago at Moody Bible Institute. We have never seen one another since. My Rising Sun had planned many things to fill the place of my extinguished tapers, but each was to be a separate and delightful discovery. Next on God's program for me was a contact which changed the whole course of my life.

CHAPTER SEVEN

J. O. FRASER OF LISULAND

WHEN AT THE CLOSE of The Firs conference in 1923, Mrs. Whipple lent me a book called *The Growth of a Soul,* she had no idea that for many years Dr. and Mrs. Isaac Page had been secretly praying that God would lay His hand on Isobel Miller for missionary service in China. She did know, however, that in the life story of Hudson Taylor, founder of the China Inland Mission, were experiences of searching for God and proving Him which were parallel to some through which I was now passing.

Anyone who knows *The Growth of a Soul* will recognize the gold mine it was to me. Hudson Taylor went much deeper in his searchings, of course, and came out with definite maxims for life and conduct. "Learn to move man, through God, by prayer alone" was one of the many that I eagerly noted, and it has blessed me all my life.

By the time I had finished the book one thing was clear to me. I wanted to belong to the Mission that Hudson Taylor founded: I wanted to work with the group who had proved God in that quiet, unostentatious fashion.

Having finished *The Growth of a Soul,* I went on

to read the second volume, *The Growth of a Word
of God*—the founding of the China Inland Mission.
It was while reading this that I received a call to
the field. Previously I had felt a call to the *Mission*
regardless of where it worked. But as I read of the
sorrows and sufferings of Chinese women my heart
was greatly stirred. I knew now what a heartache
was. When I had been groping for a way out of
spiritual darkness, my Bible was handy on my bookshelf. It was easy for me to find the way. But what
about those who had never heard of Christ? No
matter how willing they might be to follow Him
fully, if they only knew of Him and of His death for
their salvation, they must perish unless someone went
and told them. *How shall they believe in him of
whom they have not heard? and how shall they hear
without a preacher?* (Rom. 10:14). I knew I must
go and tell them. So when I arrived at The Firs in
1924, my decision to apply to the China Inland Mission had already been made.

No one needed to give up a pair of shoes to bring
me to the conference for the second time. I had been
saving money during the year, and had also applied
for the position of waitress to earn my board while
there.

I was simply thrilled to be back at the beloved
place. I ran, almost flew, from spot to spot of hal-
lowed memory. The cabin which Edna Gish (now
back in China) and I had shared, the spot in among
the tall fir trees where I had often prayed alone, the
open-air auditorium where our classes had met, the
original Firs cabin with the big fireplace where we
had held such blessed times of testimony—I wanted
to see them all. Last in my inspection tour was this
old cabin. I dashed in eagerly and was halfway to

the center of the room before I could check my impulsive entrance. For it was not empty. One lone occupant, a middle-aged gentleman, was sitting there by himself. He smiled at my surprise, and I tried to apologize while backing out as speedily as I could.

Some old bachelor, I told myself, and flew off to look at the kitchen. How I sensed that he was unmarried, I do not know. Maybe it was a certain lonely, wistful look in his eyes. Anyway, I promptly forgot him in the joy of greeting other arrivals, and getting into the swing of the waitress routine, which was new to me. Little did I dream that I had just met one who was to be a spiritual lodestar to me and to the dear husband God was planning to give me but of whose existence I, as yet, knew nothing.

It was not until the evening meeting that, to my intense surprise, I found that the "old bachelor" of the sitting-room loneliness was seated on the platform, and being introduced as our principal speaker for the conference—Mr. J. O. Fraser of the China Inland Mission. I had never heard of him before, and apparently neither had anyone else. Even Mr. Whipple probably did not know at the time that this young Englishman was an honors graduate of London University in electrical engineering, and a brilliant pianist. He appeared among us as a simple missionary, and never by word or action gave any hint of his extraordinary gifts.

When he got up to speak, he told us simply how the C.I.M. had sent him to one of the farthest corners of China, to the border of Burma and Yunnan Province. There he had worked among the Chinese for several years, but had frequently noticed a people coming into the market who were not Chinese at all. They did not speak Chinese among themselves and they did not dress like Chinese. They wore turbans and their clothing, especially that of the women, was very colorful and trimmed with cowrie shells and silver bangles. They knew some trade-language Chinese and through this he discovered that they were Lisu tribespeople who lived in the mountains of the Salween River canyon. They had never heard of the Lord Jesus Christ, and their language had never been reduced to writing—they were entirely illiterate. Moreover, they were not idol worshipers like the Chinese, but animists who worship demons. God called him to go to these people with the Gospel.

Since he was scheduled to speak several evenings during the conference, Mr. Fraser told us of a different phase of work among the Lisu each night. For instance, one night he took us itinerating over those wonderful alpine mountains, climbing great heights to where small villages perched—precariously, it often seemed!—on the edge of abysmal ravines. He told of the language difficulties—how he learned it from living with the people in their smoky little shacks, how he reduced it to writing, and how with two colleagues he was led to form what is now called the Fraser Script.

Another evening he stressed the patience needed in teaching the older folk, illiterate from their youth. He was full of humor and his descriptions of the old ladies who declared they had no power of memory, and then were tricked by him into relating with detail what had happened to their children fifteen years ago, were simply hilarious—and touching. We learned to love those old women.

One lecture was on the spiritual battle in the heavenlies. How he roughed it, and labored, and had given them a written language—and still there were

so few converts, and such as did come were not
stable. Then he wrote his mother in England to
gather in the neighbors and pray. It was only after
this prayer group began to function in earnest that
"the break" came in the Lisu tribe. At that time he
on the field had been led to resist in Christ's name
the devil and his host who were holding this tribe
enchained.

As I sat listening I saw plainly that it was true
the Lisu church was born in prayer travail, and I
decided that I must also employ this weapon of "all-
prayer." It is so obviously effective and is attainable
to any of us. I received a life-pattern at that moment
for which I have ever been grateful.

Another evening was given over to the joys of
harvest. He took us on a trip with him, and his descriptions were so vivid that we were simply transported out of America to the mountainous banks of
the Salween canyon. We saw him dressed in the
costume of a Chinese coolie, lest better clothes de-
tract from his message, with a Lisu carrier or guide,
climbing the steep approach to one of these high
villages. He cupped his hands to his mouth and
gave the Lisu call: *"Ma-pa chi la-o!"* (The male
teacher is arriving!) at which all the dogs of the village rush out and down the path at them. Then followed the banging of doors and merry shouts as the
brightly colored costumes of the women flashed back
and forth and the menfolk darted forward to drive
off the dogs. The Christians lined up to shake hands,
and as the tall missionary went down the line each
woman managed to stick an egg into his hand as she
gave the handshake of welcome! They had learned
that he liked eggs, so he always had to carry a bag

over his shoulder to hold the eggs, fresh and ancient, which such a visit collected!

He told of the Prophet's Chamber behind the chapel, which the Christian villagers built for him on learning that queerest trait of the white man, that he liked privacy sometimes! Imagine *wanting* to be alone! *Eh, eh,* how queer! Perhaps it came from the color of his skin. But if he wanted privacy he should have it. So he had a little Prophet's Chamber of his own in each village.

Then would start the catechizing for baptism. He told of going to call the next candidate and finding the man on his face, prostrate in prayer, asking his new-found Saviour to help him to answer correctly, so that he might be adjudged ready for this solemn step.

And so on.

The last night Mr. Fraser said he needed more missionaries—young men of consecration, willing for the privations and loneliness such a life entailed.

Down in my seat in the side aisle my heart thrilled with love for the Lisu people. Inwardly I prayed, "Lord, I'd be willing to go. Only I'm not a man." Never did the vision of the Lisu tribe leave me. I dared not name it a *call,* but I believe that time has proved it was.

My father was with me at The Firs that summer. And as it happened, he was Mr. Fraser's cabinmate. To my surprise, I found out that Father had invited Mr. Fraser to come and stay with us in Victoria for a week, before he sailed for China in August. That summer we had rented a house at Oak Bay, near the beach, and had room for a visitor.

I was amazed at Father's temerity in inviting Mr. Fraser without consulting Mother, because she and my brother at that time were both opposed to my going as a missionary to China. And Mother was not likely to be pleased at bringing a C.I.M. missionary into her home when she was trying to influence me to be content with Christian work in America!

But I was thrilled at the possibility of having a private talk with Mr. Fraser about missionary service. I was hoping to go to Moody Bible Institute that autumn, but the obstacles in my way were so many that I sometimes wondered if they could be from the Lord. I was Mother's only daughter: how important was that? I had made up my mind, during those evening talks on Lisuland, that this unknown missionary was a great man of God. His gifts, apart from his platform ability, were still hidden and unknown to me, but the man himself was obviously walking closely with the Lord. It was one of the thrills of my life in later years, to discover that many others, far more capable of judging such matters than I, also acclaimed him as one of the great spiritual men of his generation. He is, of course, the hero of the book, *Behind the Ranges* [1]—written many years later after his death by Mrs. Howard Taylor.

Come he did, and by his simple sincerity and kindly interest won the admiration both of my mother and brother. My mother had been a musician before her marriage. She composed music and often wrote the lyrics too, and none of her pieces had ever been refused by any publisher to whom she offered them. She did not go on with this after marriage—that was all. It was in seeking for a contact with Mother that Mr. Fraser suddenly revealed his brilliance at the piano. Mother was enthralled. They

[1] China Inland Mission, 1944.

"talked music" and Mother knew the names of his teachers and said he had been taught by some of the best masters in London.

I was watching for a chance to present my own problems, and it came later in the week. Mr. Fraser wanted to see the beach and I was appointed to take him down one afternoon. We were no sooner alone than I told him I had wanted to speak with him about my missionary call, so we sat down on the sands by a rocky bit of shore and I told him. I have never forgotten that session.

"Missionary life can be very lonely," he said quietly, and then he proceeded to unfold some of his own early sufferings. I believe now that he did it deliberately to sift me. If I were truly called of God, I would not be discouraged by plain talk about the cost. If I were not called by God, but just had romantic notions of a foreign land, the sooner my gossamer dream wafted away the better. But he little knew the unveiling of his own life that he was giving unconsciously. In fact, as he reminisced he seemed to forget for a while that I was present. His blue-grey eyes brooding out over the sunny, sparkling ocean, he seemed almost to be talking to himself. In the quiet of contemplation, as now, his eyes seemed to reveal an understanding of all the sorrows and loneliness that a human heart can know. *Acquainted with grief,* they were sad eyes; knowing the victory possible, they were *steadfast and patient.*

I told him of Mother's viewpoint and her opposition to my call. He answered with the slow drawl which was his when thinking out a question—for none could talk faster than he on occasion: "I have sensed that Satan is opposing you and working through your mother and your brother. We are taught 'whom resist' when it comes to obstacles produced by the devil. I think that should be your stand. In prayer resist the devil, always remembering to be kind to those who are unconsciously his tools at the moment: II Timothy 2:24. I have a prayer-formula which I use on such occasions. It is this: *If this obstacle be from Thee, Lord, I accept it: but if it be from Satan, I refuse him and all his works in the name of Calvary.* I have found that this formula works." I was to use it throughout my life and never found it to fail when prayed with the honest intention of obeying all that it implied.

Again Mr. Fraser brooded out over the ocean thoughtfully, then added, "I wonder if you will ever get to China. You are very young and you have great obstacles to face." He lapsed into a reverie for a few moments, then began to talk as if he knew what to say: "It is even conceivable that *after you get to Bible school,* Satan will attempt to get you away. For instance, a telegram might come saying that your mother was very sick and urging you to return home immediately. Now, if that should happen, you cannot leave the moment you get the telegram. You would have to pack your trunk and buy a ticket, and these things take time. Is there any Christian in Vancouver or here whom you can trust to be unprejudiced and yet godly enough to discern such a matter and be able to advise you?"

"There is Mr. Charles Thomson, district secretary of the C.I.M.," I answered.

"The very man!" he replied quickly. "If you get such a telegram, *wire immediately to Mr. Thomson,* asking him to check just how ill your mother is. By the time your trunk is packed you should have his reply, and can then see more clearly the path the Lord would have you take."

I listened in awe, but would have been still more amazed if I had known how exactly that prophecy was to be fulfilled.

He that is spiritual judgeth all things (I Cor. 2:15).

It was an afternoon well spent. Upon the plastic material of a young life had been imprinted standards and ideals which were to last forever. And a deep glimpse had been afforded me into the life that is hidden in God—the cost of it, the fragrance of it, and the power of it.

CHAPTER EIGHT

THE MOODY BIBLE INSTITUTE

SEPTEMBER 3, 1924, found me in Chicago, enrolling as a student of the Bible-missionary course at Moody Bible Institute. This was a most unexpected turn of affairs and not the product of my own planning. I was so very Canadian in loyalty that I would never have chosen to come to the United States for my training. And I admired Professor Ellis so much that I would not have thought of looking beyond the Vancouver Bible School for my missionary preparation. But the Lord took the matter out of my hands.

At the end of the school year 1923-4 I still lacked funds to put me through any Bible school, but outside of my parents and one other person I told no one. God in His wondrous workings brought that one other person into contact with Miss Marjorie Harrison, whom I had met at The Firs. At the precise moment she was asking Him how to use some money she had saved, and inadvertently learned that I needed funds to train for China. *It was Marjorie who chose Moody for me,* directed by the Lord, I am sure

Herself a graduate of the Bible Institute of Los Angeles, and knowing of this small Bible school right in the city where I was living, she still chose to send me halfway across the continent to Chicago. The largest school of its kind in the country, Moody Bible Institute offered rich opportunity for many kinds of Christian work. This was what I needed more than I knew.

Marjorie explained that her money was limited to that little savings account. She would buy my ticket to Chicago, but could not help me with the return fare. She would pay my board and room for one year, but had no money for my incidental expenses. And she could not help me after that first year. The Institute had an employment bureau to help students find jobs for odd hours in safe places. For the rest, I must trust the Lord. Was I willing?

Fresh from reading Hudson Taylor's experience in proving God able to supply his need through prayer only, I was thrilled with the opportunity to go on *searching*.

My brother had to make a business trip to Chicago at that time, so I had company across the continent. Dr. Isaac Page met us at the station and took me to the school. Otherwise I knew no one in that big, whirling metropolis. The Pages had but recently moved to Chicago themselves as deputation workers for the China Inland Mission in the Midwest.

That first day of enrollment, with its trips to this office and that for registration, was bewildering, and at the end of the day I was truly weary. I was put into a double room—cheaper than a single room— with a strange girl who was European and spoke with a strong accent. The furnishings were very simple, and the house opened right on the street. Being on the first floor front, we saw that people walking along the street passed right under our window. I had never lived in a house which did not have a front enclosure, and it gave me an exposed feeling to be so near a public street. This, added to weariness and loneliness, made me homesick. *Can I stand this for two years?* I was asking myself, when a bus rumbled up to a stop at our corner. To sleep with my head just the other side of a wall from such public things seemed almost scandalous. But in another moment I was swung into the heavenlies. The bus was the M.B.I. street-meeting group, returning from their first evening's witness, and they had begun to sing:

> He makes the path grow brighter
> All along the way:
> He makes the journey lighter
> Every passing day.

Beautiful young voices in four-part harmony, sung with a fervent faith in words that came right from their hearts—the singing thrilled me through and through. Something in the traffic held them there while they sang the hymn to a finish.

"Oh, Lord," I prayed in ecstasy, "thank You! Thank You! This is *the other side* of this 'exposed' existence—comradeship in the things of Christ and in the cause of soul-winning. And Christian friends who are my own age and who can sing like that? Oh, thank You, Lord!" Truly transported into His presence, I nestled down in deep content and fell asleep.

But more good things awaited me.

The next day I was called to the telephone. It was the Dean's office. "Miss Miller, there is a girl named Lillian Billington, just arrived from Bellingham, who would like to room with you. What is your pleasure in the matter?"

"Oh," I cried, "has she really come? Yes, *please*.

I would like so much to be her roommate. I met her at The Firs. She is a young schoolteacher."

"Yes, that is right," answered the office voice, "but you will have to change your dormitory. We have Miss Billington down for the third floor, Ransom Hall Building, Room 303. Will you kindly proceed to move there as soon as possible, and leave your present room in a proper state for a new occupant? Thank you. Report to us when the move is completed."

Room 303, Ransom Hall, was much larger, higher above the street, much more private, and in every way a happier arrangement to my taste. Best of all, I was to share it with a girl from The Firs. We had just met the summer before, but I liked her sweet face. "Billie" and I were happy roommates for two years. Next door at 304 was a Scottish girl, Anne Barr—who years later was to be namesake to my daughter—and a very unselfish American girl, Ella Dieken, who was later to play a part in my life that the wildest dreams could never have conjured up.

What a meeting Billie and I had! And what fun to help her unpack and find that she had things I didn't —pretty curtains for our windows, cretonne drapes for our trunks, lacy dresser scarfs, and so on. Soon our room was transformed into a real girls' bower, and my beauty-loving soul was deeply grateful.

Mealtime was an adventure, with hundreds of students all eating at once. Oh the noise of the talk, the clatter of the cutlery and dishes! The men sat on one side of the dining room and the women on the other, twelve to a table. A senior and a junior student were assigned to the end seats, but the rest of us changed places each day. Two students at each table were appointed daily to bring in the food and carry the dishes out.

I was waiting in line one day for the hot vegetables. As soon as the bell rang, the food would be dished out to us, but there was still a moment before the hour struck. I was dreaming of Lisuland when, turning around suddenly, I encountered the eyes of another dreamer—the young man who ran the dishwashing machine. It was one of those shock-encounters when you find yourself already over the threshold and into the other fellow's soul before there is time to knock for admission. Very embarrassing. Each of us looked away quickly and pretended not to notice, but it had happened. From then on I was conscious of that dishwasher! Whether he was a full-time kitchen employee or student-help I did not know. The annoying thing was that I had become conscious of him.

Now I had made up my mind that I was not going to have any boy friends at Moody. I had proved that they were distracting and I wanted these two years to be given to unhindered preparation for my life-work in China. So I was extremely cross with myself to find out that as soon as I entered the kitchen I looked every time to see if he was there or not. To discipline myself, I did not inquire his name or his status, but frequently I had to carry dishes past him and I felt sure he knew my name and all about me.

And I was correct: he did. But he never tried to speak. I did appreciate that. I did not know that he had come to the Bible Institute vowing to have nothing to do with girls—lest they distract him from *his* studies! But he had made inquiries as to who the girl was who wore the green blouse trimmed with brown swan's down.

Shortly after my arrival, Dr. and Mrs. Page invited me to supper in their apartment. He had long been my father's close friend and I had called him Daddy Page for years. After I had taken off my wraps, he thrust a bundle of photographs of the Institute and Moody students into my hands, excusing himself while he went to help his wife in the kitchen. As I looked over the pictures I came across one which greatly attracted me—the portrait of a girl that showed character as well as beauty.

"Oh, Daddy Page," I cried, "who is this? What a lovely face! Is she here at the Institute?"

He came in and looked over my shoulder. "Oh that," he said. "Yes, Isobel. She *is* a lovely girl. Her name is Kathryn Kuhn, but she has just graduated and gone on to Wheaton College. I wish you could meet her. She has a brother here at the Institute."

"Oh, yes?" I said politely, and quickly changed the conversation. But inwardly I said, *Well, if her brother looks like she does, I'll stay away from him. Here's where you don't go to any mixed parties, Isobel Miller!*

Apart from the freshman reception, I quietly refused invitations to any party or picnic where young men would be present—that is, during my first term. It was my second term before I found out all this reserve had been in vain, for I learned that the dishwasher in the kitchen was the brother of Kathryn Kuhn!

Of my studies during those two years and four months—I was ill and lost a term—I can only glance at the blessing they brought me. Dr. James Gray was President then and I was privileged to have a class under him. Bible Analysis under Dr. Robert Jader-

quist was an outstanding joy, and I later passed it
on to the Lisu church, analyzing First and Second
Peter with our Bible School students. Those notes
are still being used.

Dr. Elbert McCreery taught Comparative Reli-
gions and was one of my favorite teachers. He was
himself the blessing, with his gentle, Christ-like life.

Dr. Robert Hall Glover made me sit on the edge
of my seat in eagerness, week after week, as he presented the challenge of missions, and in another class
taught the History of Missions. His fire continually
enkindled my own.

Talmage J. Bittikofer taught us part-singing and
conducting, which I was to use constantly with the
Lisu church. We all loved "Bitti" and his solos
stirred me to the depths.

So I could go on, but I think the greatest help
came to me at Moody in the practical work assignments, under the direction of Mrs. Frances C. Allison. Every student had to take one or more assignments each week; and these assignments were
changed each term, giving every student a great
variety of experience. Open-air meetings among the
Jews would likely mean rotten eggs and tomatoes
pelted at you, so you wore your oldest clothes. (I was
knocked off the pavement into the street once when
my turn came for Jewish work). Sunday school
classes and hospital or jail visitation were considered
the easiest assignments, and my Lord started me off
gently with these. A slip of paper from the Practical
Work Department told me I was assigned to teach a
Sunday school class and do visitation during the week
in the Italian slums. I would work under senior
student Miss Ethel Thompson, Room X, 830 Build-

ing, and would I please report to her immediately for instructions.

So behold a young Moody freshman climbing the stairs of the 830 Building and standing before a closed bedroom door, about to knock. What would Miss Thompson be like? How could I ever do slum visitation? How my heart beat as I firmly knocked at that door! Once it opened, I was in for it—that is, I must plunge into soul-winning, from which my shyness had always shrunk.

The door was opened by a short, slim young woman, perhaps in her early thirties, who, when she heard my name, welcomed me quickly with a soft, southern drawl in her voice. After asking me to sit down, she began: "I suppose I had better tell you about our assignment. We are working under a community house or church in the Italian quarter. The minister in charge is a modernist and conducts dances on Sunday evening, and so on. This is our big difficulty and the most discouraging feature. But we are in charge of the Primary Department on Sundays and have full liberty to preach the Gospel there. They think we cannot 'hurt' the little ones!

"During the week we go into the homes—tenement houses—knock at doors, and present our message. The people are poor, of course, and many of them are Roman Catholics, but there have been a few decisions for Christ. Personally, I think the work needs prayer almost more than anything else."

"Tommy" (none of the students called her Ethel) eyed this new freshman questioningly, wondering what the Lord had sent her in me.

Remembering Mr. Fraser's lessons on the place of prayer in Christian service, I answered eagerly, "Oh, I believe in prayer too! I'd be happy to come over

here to your room every day for a time of prayer
together."

"Would you?" said Tommy, her face lighting up
with hope and joy. "All right. I'm working my way
through school here, so I am busy, but half an hour
before noon each day—how would that suit you?"
It fit into my schedule and became an important
part of my life.

That first Sunday Tommy took me to the community center and introduced me to the Rev. Mr.
K——, the minister in charge, as her new helper.
"Fine," he said, "how about having lunch with us
today? I told the wife there would be a new worker
and we ought to get acquainted—so she is prepared."

That meant our staying for the morning service.
Mr. K—— spoke about courage or high ideals or
gave some such verbal essay, but there was nothing
in it to bring new life to anyone.

After dinner in their apartment, he said to us
rather patronizingly, "You know, girls, I used to
believe like you do. In fact, you may be surprised
to learn that I am a Bible school graduate myself.
But after graduation I went into a seminary and
there learned that no one nowadays believes in that
old-fashioned stuff. I lost my 'faith,' as you call it,
at seminary. But somehow our liberalism does not
energize people like your teaching seems to, so when
I found out how dead the work is here, I asked for
a couple of Moody students to be sent us, to stir up
interest in the neighborhood. You bring them in,
and we'll mold them into a good community!"

We stifled the comment that rose so quickly to our
lips, and I said, "This is very strange, Mr. K——.
You have departed from the old faith and I have just
departed from liberalism to return to the faith! I lost

my belief in God in college, but I have done some
personal investigation in the matter and I'm now
convinced that He is, and the only way to Him is
through faith in the atoning power of the blood of
Christ to bring forgiveness of sins and eternal life.
You and I are a contrasting pair—you have entered
The Misty Flats while I have just found my way out
of them back on to the High Way again."

Mr. K——'s eyes sparkled with interest, and he
leaned forward, plying me with questions. He was
sarcastic and argumentative, but evidently moved.
Tommy sat quiet, praying. She had never heard my
story, but recognized instantly the working of the
Spirit of God.

When it came time to leave, Mr. K—— was belligerent again. "You're too intelligent a girl to slip
back into that old stuff," he challenged me. "We'll
have to have some more talks about this! You girls
must come to supper some night after your visitation
work."

On the long car ride home Tommy said, "I believe God has already begun to answer our prayers.
Just think of His sending a worker who had been
through all this liberal stuff that is binding this man
from any power really to help change lives! I watched
his face while you talked and many of your points
went home, though he was too proud to acknowledge
it. I have faith now to believe that God will bring
Mr. K—— back to the faith! Let us agree together
on Matthew 18:19 [1] and add this request to our
daily prayers."

---

[1] "Again I say unto you, That if two of you shall
agree on earth as touching any thing that they shall ask,
it shall be done for them of my Father which is in
heaven" (Matt. 18:19).

Tommy proved to be a most rare companion. She had a keen sense of humor, and droll wit simply poured from her. Visitation was in itself a grim experience for me. Those dark, dirty tenement houses, with broken stairs, bad plumbing which often made the place reek, and whole families cooped up in one small room sometimes, would have terrified me if I had been alone. But Tommy always had a merry retort or comment for a stubbed toe or an offended nose—a remark so pungent in its truth and applicability that I was shaken with laughter which often helped me to overcome my distaste. She always took the brunt of the first attack, so to speak. She was an artist at tactful approach, and I sat at her feet and tried to learn. More than thirty years have passed since those days, so I cannot remember details of her personal work conversations or of her delightful wit. But I do remember one incident. In a long, dark hall of an old tenement house we were going from door to door, seeking entrance and opportunities for conversation. One door was opened by a big brute of a man who scowled at us and shouted, "What are you after? What ya doin' here?"

"Brother," smiled up Tommy at him with her soft, southern drawl, "we're a couple of friends who are interested in seeing that you get a better deal. Won't you let us come in and talk a moment?"

"Ah, come on," growled the man suspiciously. "Nobody's really interested in helping us. What's your line? Salesman? Politics? Whatever it is, we ain't interested," and he moved to the door as if to bang it in our faces.

"Now, brother," piped up Tommy plaintively, "a pair of poor tired girls can't hurt a big fellow like you. Won't you even offer us a chair a moment?

We've been on our feet for hours and we did hope——" A woman's voice came from within: "They can sit down a moment, can't they, Bill? I know what it is to have tired feet."

Bill cursed bitterly, but left the door open; then he turned and stalked to the far side of the dismal room. Tommy, with a droll remark about her feet, made the woman laugh, and a conversation was soon under way. The Lord's name was no sooner uttered, however, than Bill appeared in our midst again, eyes blazing with anger. "So it's religious sluts you are! That's the worst of all! I'm not going to have any blankety blank"—he swore profusely—"whinings around here! I'm an atheist, I am"—and so on.

Tommy turned on her loving, merry humor. I do not know how she did it, except that the Spirit of God was working with her, but she had him quieted and listening before we left. If I remember rightly, his wife decided for Christ. Almost every visitation day, some soul made that decision for eternity. Dear Tommy—it was she who taught me that "loving folks" is the only way to approach them for the Lord Jesus Christ.

In the Primary Department of the church, also, God began to work. The children started to ask the Lord to come into their hearts. Mr. K—— was interested and indifferent by turns. Sometimes he would ignore us for weeks, almost as if antagonistic. On other occasions he would come into our Sunday school, listen and watch, and invite us around for a meal.

How we labored in prayer for this man! Tommy with her cute remarks in the dark hallways of tenement houses was one person; on her knees praying for the salvation of souls and the reclamation of Mr

K——, she was quite a different person, yet the two sides of her character blended into one another. If you heard only her jokes, you would never have guessed at her tears and her passionate pleadings for sin-bound souls.

In my second term I asked to be reappointed to the same assignment, as Tommy and I both felt the Lord's work was not completed in that place. But that was the term I fell ill and lost six weeks of study, and of course could not go with Tommy. At the end of that term she graduated and left for Mexico.

But there is one precious thing yet to record.

After I came out of the infirmary and just before Tommy left the Institute, we were both called down to the reception room one day. To our surprise, it was Mr. K——. He was a changed man and his face wore a gentle, chastened look, and there was a light there we had never seen before.

"I am calling on you girls to tell you that the Lord has answered your prayers for me," he said. "I have come back to Him. It has been a bitter fight, as you doubtless have watched and seen. Pride refused to be crucified for a long time. But week by week it became more evident to me that the Word you girls preached was the power of God unto salvation. Lives were changed through your ministry; my honesty had to admit it. Nobody was changed through mine. Maybe you don't know that I began to preach the Bible again when I saw how God used your Bible teaching. But nothing happened. Then I had to come to the place where I was willing to preach the cross of Christ as the *only* way, the blood of the Redeemer as the *only* atonement for our sins. The preaching of the cross *worked*—for me as well as for you. There has been an awful fuss. I made a confession in the pulpit and stopped the Sunday dances. Attendance picked up, the church was filled for services, but the committee got wind of what I had done and were very angry." Tears came into his eyes. "In short, they dismissed me, but I have a little country church appointment now and will be moving out there with my family. And I can preach the truth there. My wife is wholeheartedly with me and we both feel we have to thank you two. God bless you. And *God bless the school that D. L. Moody founded.*"

With tears in our eyes and awe in our hearts we said a hearty "Amen."

We did not see Mr. K—— again.

CHAPTER NINE

SPIRITUAL PREVISION

IN DECEMBER 1924 I received a letter from my mother saying that she was facing the possibility of undergoing a surgical operation. It was discovered that she had a tumor and there was a choice before her: radiology treatments over quite a long period of time, or surgery. She was inclined toward surgery as being less drawn out—to get it over with instead of making the many long trips to town which the radiology would necessitate. I had not heard definitely what her decision had been when a telegram arrived saying she was with the Lord. She had chosen surgery and had died in the hospital following the operation. Father wired me lovingly, but said the funeral would be over before I could reach home, so I should not try to come.

This was a shattering blow to me. My mother had opposed my going to the foreign field because of her clinging love for me, her only daughter. In the agony of her pleadings with me she had said some bitter things which at the time I had not taken to heart, as I recognized they were the upflinging of violent emotion and not the result of considered thought. But one word had been: "You are praying to go to China, and God answers prayer, but you will go only over my dead body." Of course, that memory now came back to me and simply lacerated my heart.

I owe a great deal to my mother. With her deep affections she held high ideals and was very conscientious. She sacrificed her musical career and many opportunities for a musical evening with other young people in order to baby-sit with her two children at home. She married young and was still in her twenties when my brother and I were born. She had great ambitions for her children and carefully watched over us. We were never allowed to run the streets. She gave up her evenings to reading to us and planning to make home a pleasant place where our friends were welcome. She was a Christian, at one time a consecrated Christian, and always trained us to love the Lord and honor His Word. As we grew older she wanted us "to move in good society," and this was the temptation which had led her to compromise with worldly things. But at the root of it was her natural love for us.

I took my mother's love for granted, accepting the warmth of the daily sunshine in such careless security that I had not shown her the gratitude which was her due. All these things came back to me now that she was gone, but it was too late to express my thanks to her and my heart was sorely torn.

During that Christmas vacation I took employment as a waitress in a restaurant. School reopened in January.

One day in class a messenger went up to the platform and handed the teacher a note. He read it and said: "Will Miss Isobel Miller please go to the office of the Dean of Women? There is a telegram for you."

Astounded and wondering, I got up and sped toward the Women's Building. What could it be? I was trembling by the time I reached the office, and from the Dean's face I knew it was bad news of some kind. I could only look at her in agony and beg that she tell me quickly and not prolong suspense. She did so, "Sit down, dear. The telegram reads: FATHER CRITICALLY INJURED IN ELEVATOR ACCIDENT. COME HOME AT ONCE. MURRAY. Who is Murray?"

"My brother," I choked. "Oh, but I can't stand it. Father too! Oh——!"

"Is there anyone we can call to help you, dear?" she asked tenderly.

Suddenly in imagination I was far away, sitting on a seaside beach beside a tall, strong man who was looking out over the breaking sea with brooding eyes, and he was saying, "Satan may try to get you away from the Institute. Is there anyone you know who can be depended on for godly, unprejudiced judgment?" In a flash I recognized that Mr. Fraser's foresight had been an exact premonition in all except one detail. He had thought it would be Mother, but it turned out to be my brother who summoned me home. The memory of Mr. Fraser's advice steadied and quieted me.

Sitting up straight, I said, "Yes, please. I would like Dr. Isaac Page to come and help me."

The dean was relieved to be able to do something, and in a moment she was talking to him on the telephone. I heard him say, "I'll take a taxi and be there immediately." I waited in the dean's office until he arrived—my father's intimate friend.

"Daddy Page," I said, "Mr. Fraser told me this might happen. He also told me what to do if it did happen. I will go and pack my trunk, but will you please do two things for me? Reserve a ticket for the train tonight, but don't buy it yet. Will you please wire immediately to Mr. Charles Thomson and ask if Dad is as bad as Murray said?"

"Excellent idea, Isobel," said Dr. Page. "First reports of these accidents are often excited and exaggerated. Mr. Thomson will know. I will go and do that immediately—there is no train going to Vancouver until this evening, anyway. And you? You will trust and not be afraid?"

"Yes," I said, much calmer now that a plan of activity was under way. "Thank you. Everyone here is so kind and loving to me. I will be all right."

"I'll come back just as soon as I have wired and made the train reservation," he said, and was gone.

Before supper that evening the answering telegram arrived. It read: FATHER IMPROVING SENDS LOVE AND SAYS STAY AT YOUR POST. WRITING. THOMSON.

Oh, what a relief! The letter that followed told how the elevator girl had lost control and the cage had crashed four stories to the cement basement. Daddy was injured internally and the jar began a trouble which did finally take his life, but he lived for nearly twenty happy years before that took place!

"He that is spiritual judgeth all things" (I Cor. 2:15).

How did Mr. Fraser know this might happen? When God's child is living close to Him and perfectly yielded to His Will, it is possible to spread his mind out in the Lord's presence and catch the instruction of God, especially if interceding for someone else. If there were no God this could not be. Satan can read man's thought and describe the past; he can use intelligence and *guess* at the future, but he cannot *know* the future.

This experience was followed closely by another special instance of the Spirit's operation.

The Otis Whipple family were no longer in Seattle, but in China. Mr. Whipple, a fine architect, had been called to build a missionary hospital in one of the big inland cities. He took his family with him, so it was some time before Mrs. Whipple heard of my sorrows.

One day I received a letter from her. It said something like this. "Isobel, I feel your mother was spiritually prepared to go home. It was very strange. I knew nothing of the possibility of her operation, let alone her danger, but on the day of her death I was so burdened for her that I spent a long time in prayer and had assurance that she was at last yielded to God's will in all things.

"But now as I write I have another burden that presses upon me. It is for you, and somehow connected with your father. I am in much prayer for you, dear, and for him. I do not know what is happening, but God has called me today to intercede for you both, and claim only His will to be done upon each of you."

I looked at the date of Mrs. Whipple's letter. It was the very day the telegram came telling of Father's accident. Mrs. Whipple was in inland China, halfway around the world, with no human knowledge whatever of what had taken place. She could not possibly have known, for I did not learn it myself for several months, that before she went to the hospital Mother admitted that I had chosen the better course in pursuing the will of God. What had been worldly ambition in her life she confessed to Him and before she died she came back to her earlier consecration of all to the Lord. And who knows how much

Mrs. Whipple's intercession helped to win that battle?

I was deeply impressed, wistfully wondering if I would ever attain to the place where God could trust me with His counsels in this way. I did not know that God has these gifts in greater or less measure for all who are born again of the Spirit and living in obedience to that Holy Spirit. I was soon to learn.

Joy at Father's recovery was quickly followed by a new anxiety. Mother had been the business head in the family and it was she who had managed to make ends meet, and who had planned so carefully that I was able to get an education. Father was of Micawber's optimistic and gullible temperament. He was always going to "strike it rich" by investment in copper, silver, or gold mines, or some such venture. The fact that he had consistently lost all his life savings in these "promising" stocks never seemed to teach him. After Mother's death I was perturbed to hear that Father had given up his profession and had gone in for stock-selling—this time a new invention which would make us all millionaires in a short time! Brother, too, had sold his chicken ranch, and apparently was not working at anything. Why start something new if you are going to be independently wealthy soon? They rented a little bungalow in North Vancouver, sold some of our furniture, and moved the rest in. These cheerful, wonderful-sounding letters only served to burden me: the higher Daddy's expectations rose, the lower sank my heart!

"Lord, is life to be always grim?" I whispered to Him. His answer was not long in coming.

It was in General Missions class that Dr. Glover repeated a previous announcement. "I have told you before," he said, "of the Foreign Missions Convention of the United States and Canada to be held in Washington, D.C., January 28 to February 2. The Moody Bible Institute has been allotted eight delegates, but we only have six signed up to go. This will be a wonderful experience, since famous missionaries and native converts from all over the world are coming. President Coolidge is to open the session. I am sure there are some in the student body who can afford to pay their own way. The time is getting short. I would urge you to sign up. Next week is the last opportunity, so get ready."

Delegate to a great missionary conference in our nation's capital! My heart reached out in longing to go. Suddenly I felt I was to go. It was as if the Lord said, "You had a long enough siege of sorrow, dear. I'm going to send you to Washington for a little time of joy." I thrilled through and through and believed Him. Yet it was an impossible hope. I had not a cent to put toward the expense. All week long I imagined the Lord sending me a huge gift of money and my trotting up to Dr. Glover and offering to be a delegate—but not a cent came in.

The last day of opportunity arrived. At Missions class that morning several student volunteers had been asked to speak three minutes each, telling why they felt they should go to the foreign field, and at the end Dr. Glover again made an impassioned plea for one more delegate to the Washington Conference. The opportunity would close that night, he said. I left the class wondering if it had been the voice of the Lord I heard, or had I been deceived by wishful thinking? That noon there was a note in my mailbox. *Call at Dr. Glover's office immediately,* it read. With high-bounding heart I simply ran to the building where the Director of Missions had his office and, trembling with excitement, knocked at the door. "Come in! . . . Oh, Miss Miller, sit down," Dr. Glover beamed at me. "I sent for you to tell you that someone has offered to pay your way to the conference. Would you like to go?"

"Oh," I gasped. *"Would I?* But who could the donor be?" I wondered if perhaps Dr. and Mrs. Page might have offered this help, but how could they afford it?

"The donor wishes to remain unknown," Dr. Glover replied, "and I believe she is a stranger to you." He had said *she,* so I knew it was a woman! He went on: "She has paid your fare, your hotel fees, and meals, and has added an extra twenty dollars just for fun. Here it is. The rail fare and hotel bill I'll pay for you. Now you'll have to be ready to leave by tomorrow. Can you make it? I already have permission for you from the Dean of Women."

I made it, all right!

But I would like to tell you how God worked this out for me, for the dear benefactress did allow me to know the story later on. She was a well-to-do Christian recently widowed. That Thursday morning she happened to be downtown on business near the Institute, and, glancing at her watch, saw there was time to slip in and listen to Dr. Glover's Missions Hour. As she slipped into a seat among the students, I was called up to give my testimony. When I had finished, Mrs. X—— whispered to the girl seated next to her, "Who was that speaker?" We neither of us knew who that girl was, but she told not only my name but also added, "Isobel has been going through deep sorrow. Her mother died before Christmas and a few weeks later her father was nearly killed in an

accident." The kind little widow's heart went ou'
to me, her own bereavement still fresh upon her, so
when Dr. Glover arose to make a last plea for the
one remaining delegate, she felt instantly that she
would like to send me. "A change of scene, inspiring
messages, sightseeing around the capital," she
thought, "is just what that girl needs. I'll give it to
her, and incidentally Moody Bible Institute can have
its full quota of delegates."

God bless His generous stewards who live in the
flow of His thoughts, so that He can think and act
through them.

Such spiritual premonitions I never had before I
found the Lord. From time to time I have had them
ever since. I believe they are given for the purpose
of comfort and to refresh our experience that *He is
there,* and that He cares. Only God could have
worked out that little forecast and fulfillment.

And so began one of the high peaks of joy which
tower up exultantly above the painful valley experiences of my life. It was one that has always been
outstanding, and it molded my life as I little suspected it would have any power to do, for one of the
other eight delegates was John B. Kuhn.

I had been formally introduced to him at last,
and it was at a mixed party after all! The occasion
was Daddy Page's birthday, when a group of young
Student Volunteers whom the Pages had often had
at their home decided to give him a surprise party.
I was told there would be boys present and also that
one of these would be the brother of Kathryn Kuhn,
so I knew I was to meet him at last. But how could
I get out of it? If it had been the birthday of a member of the staff, for instance, I could have found an

excuse. But my own dear Daddy Page—I just *had* to go to his birthday party!

The group was to meet at half-past seven on the corner of Clark Street, where we caught the street car. We girls arrived first, and the moon was rising over the tall old houses when we saw the group of boys approaching. "Oh, here they come!" cried the leader of us girls. "Miss Miller, let me introduce Jack Graham and John Kuhn and—" I heard no more. I found myself looking straight into the face of—the dishwasher from the Bible Institute kitchen!

It was a wonderful convention, with world-renowned missionaries taking part. We heard them speak and met some of them personally. Between meetings we went sightseeing. We visited the White House and were presented to President Coolidge, shaking hands with him. After it was over we all had a short trip to Mount Vernon to see the home of George and Martha Washington. What good times we had—sitting together, eating together, sightseeing through snow-slushy Washington, laughing and teasing when we set out to buy Gordon Hedderly Smith some rubbers, only to hear the clerk say they did not carry such a large size!

How little we knew of what future years would hold—that two of the delegates would marry each other and serve Him in far-off Lisuland, that Jack Graham would serve in the same province, ministering to the Miao tribe, that Irene Forsythe would have a wonderful ministry in Shantung among the Chinese, that Gordon Smith would open up work among many new tribes in Indo-China. Friendships were formed during those delegate days that have sweetened the whole road of life ever since.

CHAPTER TEN

AT SUNDRY TIMES AND IN DIVERS MANNERS

WHEN IS THE SEARCH ENDED? In one sense, it is finished when our hand, stretched out to God in the name of His appointed mediator Jesus Christ feels the answering grasp and knows that He is there. But in another sense the searching never ends, for the first discovery is quickly followed by another, and that by another—and so it goes on.

As I write it is dawning a new day. The far horizon has seen the bright spot of the rising sun, but heavy clouds soon covered it. These clouds have become illuminated and streaks of pink and gold beauty are breaking through chance rents in their filmy cover. Glory after glory appears as the eye eagerly explores the heavens. And so it is with God. To find that He is, this is the mere starting-point of our search. We are lured on to explore *what* He is, and that search is never finished, for it grows more thrilling the further one proceeds.

Up to this point I have discovered that God is, and that He is mine by the mediatorship of Christ. I have discovered that He can and will teach me His way, or His plan for my life. I have found that He can overcome obstacles and that we do not need to arouse a great hullabaloo to get Him to do so. Hudson Taylor was right in his discovery: "Learn to move man, through God, by prayer alone." *By searching* I have discovered that God has strange and sweet ways of manifesting Himself, at sundry times and in divers manners He is still speaking. He is just as versatile in caring for the needs of those who trust Him, and in this chapter I am going to tell how He provided for me in different ways at different times. I have already told how, through Marjorie Harrison, God provided my fare to Chicago and board and room at the Institute for one year. I have also told of His remarkable provision for my trip to Washington. How He made provision for the autumn term of 1925, when Marjorie's money had all been used up and I was entirely dependent on my own earnings is another story of God's care. It involves another life which had touched mine the previous spring.

It must have been about April, 1925, that I was struck by a prayer request given in the evening devotions hours. A graduate student got up and asked prayer for "a girl friend who has suffered a terrible tragedy and has lost her faith. She is coming to see me at the Institute. Pray she may find the Lord again."

A girl, struck by heartbreak, pushed onto The Misty Flats and was floundering bitterly—I saw it all with a sympathy that pierced my heart. *Lord, give her to me,* I prayed inwardly. *Oh, I can understand how she feels!* I felt He answered that He would.

Humanly speaking, there was no likelihood of our meeting in the ordinary course of events. I was now working part-time as a noon rush-hour waitress, and the graduate student who had given the request moved in a different circle. "The élite" we laughingly dubbed those students who were wealthy enough to go through school without working their way. They had plenty of leisure and we had none, so "the élite" and "the workers" seldom met outside of classrooms. They had picnics and parties for which we could not afford the time and naturally each group clanned together. I could have pushed my way up to the graduate student and asked for an introduction and would have been nicely received, but I decided that if it were of the Lord, He must work it out in His own way. Then I would know that it was not my own impulsive wishing. I prayed about it.

The strange thing is that neither Ruth nor I can remember how it came about. I have a dim recollection of a chance encounter in the post office. I was watching the élite set for the appearance of a stranger, so spotted her early. She was tall and slim, with naturally curly light brown hair, and the soft accent of a Southerner. But why she noticed me among the hundreds of unfamiliar girl-faces at the Institute, I will never know. God answered my prayer and "gave" me Ruth—that is all I need to say.

Soon she was coming to our room for talks and pursuing me wherever she could catch this student laborer. I remember once encountering her just before the noon hour, when I was rushing off to be waitress at that restaurant—the employees' restaurant of a large corporation near by.

"I want to talk to you!" she said.

"Fine," I answered. "Can you come in tonight? I'm on my way to work now and dare not stop—I'll just barely make it."

"No!" she replied petulantly. "I want to talk *now*.

I'll walk with you to your job—nothing against that, is there, ma'am?" (We had great fun over the difference in Canadian and Southern speech-forms. To me, *ma'am* was the language of a servant to a mistress; to her it was the polite way to apologize. She laughed much and mimicked drolly my *I beg your pardon?* and rubbed in her *ma'am* as often as possible with a teasing sparkle in her eyes.)

Now I was just a little diffident about Ruth seeing me in that restaurant. I was servant to the servants there, so to speak, and the rush-hour girls had to take left-over apron uniforms, usually very ill-fitting ones. Ruth was the only child of well-to-do people, and cultured homes were her natural environment. What would she say if she saw me in that restaurant? But she was quick to notice my slight hesitation in accepting her escort, and nothing would shake her off from that moment. Right into the restaurant she came and saw it all—saw, too, my embarrassment, and mischievously determined to make the most of it.

Ruth was the twentieth-century counterpart of Mary Tudor—sister of Henry VIII. Charming, capricious, affectionate, and utterly lovable, clever and nimble-witted, she was still untamed. To use a more vulgar but more explicit word, she was *unspanked*. Her parents had spared the rod, and that kind of upbringing always follows a child through the rest of life.

It was impossible ever to "handle" Ruth. She saw you tuck the handle under your apron just as soon as you moved your arm, and with an almost devilish mischief she would whisk it out and brandish it before your chagrined face and defy you. She was my superior in personality, brains, social culture—in everything but one thing. She did not possess the fellowship of the Lord Jesus Christ or know Him as I did—and that was what I longed that she might. But I had not been with her long before I knew that I could never "deal" with her. She was too quick to recognize any such effort, and she had my own resentment at the invasion of her spiritual sanctum. She would open it up when and where she liked, but no one should knock it open. The only thing I knew to do was to love her and pray for her.

Somewhere along the line—maybe an evening session, relaxed on her bed, talking in the dark—she suddenly opened up and told me her tragedy. She had become engaged to one of God's finest gentlemen, one who knew Him and served Him devoutly. But they had quarreled and Ruth had high-handedly broken their engagement. She had never meant really to break with Jack, for she loved him too dearly for that. But she had conceived a pique against life for disappointing her, and had to take it out on someone. At the first overture Jack might make she would melt and be his own darling Ruth again—that was her inward thought. But no overture came. She did not know that even while she had this tiff with him, he was going down with a fever. When she did learn of it, he was already in Heaven.

After this she had an unfortunate experience with a religious hypocrite, and with her lightning-like petulance had said that she could not believe in God when a Christian would act like that.

Yes, it is better to have the rod when you are a child. When life must wield it against you, it is too cruel. Can you think what her agonies were? Not just to have lost him—their wedding date had been set—

but to have him go before she was able to say, "Oh, I did not mean it! I'm sorry. Please forgive me."

Her kind, worldly father did the best he knew. He handed her his check-book and said, "Go to New York and have a good time. Forget the irrevocable." She went, and all the wild life she led I did not care to hear about. One question was making my heart stand still: "Ruth, did you not grope for the low road?"

She was silent a moment. "I know what you mean. No. Somehow there has always been in me a hidden passion for chastity. But everything else I did—I was wild."

I sighed a *Thank God!* Christ can save from the low road, where a man "wallows in fleshly things until his appetites become fibrous," as praise God our city rescue missions all testify. As for the hidden passion for chastity, I understood that too.

> Hast thou heard Him, seen Him, known Him?
> Is not thine a captured heart?

Anyone who has ever really known the Lord, even only in reflection, can never again be satisfied with less.

"Did the check-book and New York's wildest— *help?*" I asked.

She withered me with a look. "You know it didn't."

How I prayed for this dear, honest, if willful young life. I thought I had been able to help her out from The Misty Flats, but later she was sucked back in again. She is His now, however. In my Moody autograph book—which is a large tome—her autograph covers four pages, written in three installments. The first is one of her nonsense poems, shrewd with

perspicuity. (She has a literary gift, among other
things. The élite publishing houses reach after her
manuscripts! They do not even know that I exist.)

The third installment reads:

> Wonder if I'll ever finish this—sounds like The
> Perils of Ruth in three installments. What I've
> been trying to say for the last two pages is that
> I love you (just plain, unadulterated, simple-
> minded love). You have meant so very much to
> me—you, yourself—and you have meant infinitely
> more in that you have both *showed* me the way
> and *fought with* me during these hard days of de-
> cision. I can wish no greater thing than that you
> may mean just that to these dear folks in China.

I know that Ruth had been "sifting" me. When
she caught a glimpse of pride wincing, she seized on
it and walked right to the restaurant to see every bit
of it. More than that, at a later date, without any
warning she brought a college girl friend with her to
that same restaurant to catch me as I was.

But she did more than sift. Tenderly affectionate
and generous, she discovered that I enjoyed beautiful
things. Maybe it began by her getting permission
from the dean to take me out for a meal—so we
would have that much more time to talk. My frank
delight in the harmonious drapes, shaded lights, and
soft classical dinner music amused Ruth. From then
on she deliberately hunted up quaint, pretty tearooms and increased the frequency of her invitations.
With her unfailing charm, she could wangle a permission out of a dean that no one else would even
dare to propose. And so she "embroidered" my days.

But her careless use of money shocked me. When
away from Chicago she once sent me a telegram in
lieu of a letter. When I remonstrated by letter I re-

ceived a second telegram to laugh at me! No, you could not "handle" Ruth!

But there came a day when, to her astonishment, she found that someone else could be hard to handle too. The summer of 1925 I spent in Canada with my Aunt Nellie, Mother's younger sister. On returning to the Institute I now faced having to support myself entirely. This meant working three times a day instead of only at noon, but I was highly favored, for I had obtained the post of waitress at the faculty table in the Institute dining room. This meant being down half an hour before each meal in order to prepare the food nicely, and it meant staying half an hour afterward to wash up and set the table, and then there was the time consumed in having my meal after the other students had already finished theirs. It was not too strenuous, however, for it was work among Christians—no more heathen Americans shouting at me. It was exacting, for I had to be there right on time, but it was no great distance away, such as the other job had been. No time was wasted in getting to work.

One day I was in the act of preparing a meal when in breezed Ruth. She had arrived unexpectedly with her parents for a short visit. "So this is what we are now!" she teased. "Say, I've got something to tell you." With an eye on the clock hand which was traveling close toward my deadline, I said, "Keep it, dearie, until tonight—can you? I'm dying to hear it, but my job has to come first. I have to get this finished before the faculty arrives. I'm working full-time this term." There would be no more meals out in pretty tearooms.

Ruth stood and pouted. "But I want to talk to you about my soul!" she said with a twinkle in her eye.

"How important is *that?* And you stand there flaying radishes into rosebuds and say, 'Another time.' How do you know I'll feel like talking about it at another time? There is something wrong here. Something's got to be done about this." Then she had to leave because the faculty were already beginning to arrive.

I felt very uncomfortable. It was true that Ruth wasn't the kind of person who could open up the doors of her sanctum at any odd moment. On the other hand, I had to work, and surely the Lord expected faithfulness in my job. Inwardly I prayed for help and went on with the task in hand.

Ruth was busy too. She arrived in my room that evening her old gay self. "I have it all arranged!" she said happily. "No more table-serving for Little Pats!" That was her pet name for me. (Apparently I am addicted to short, quick movements when showing affection—many short, little kisses, and many little pats on the back in a hug. My children laugh at the former and Ruth declared she got homesick for the latter—and the name has pursued me through the years.)

"I told my father about you, and he says he will be delighted to support you through the rest of your schooling here. Now then! Whenever Ruthie arrives and needs talking to, she can have it. And many others too. Don't you see the Lord's hand in this— *ma'am?*"—with roguish delight. But I didn't, and there was an awkward silence. Ruth's father was a fine, clean man, but he played the races and gained his money in the usual worldly ways. Hudson Taylor believed firmly that God does not need, and will not use for blessing, money offered by unbelievers. God is able to provide for His own children apart from help from those who serve Mammon. "We can af-

ford to have as little as the Lord chooses to give,"
he once said, "but we cannot afford to have *unconsecrated money.*" But would Ruth ever be able to
understand what I meant by refusing on that score?
Her eyes sparkled with mischievous delight when I
said her father's money was *unconsecrated*—she
would have a good time telling him that! Miserably,
I tried to explain without appearing ungrateful. But
when she saw that it really touched what was sacred
to me, she accepted it quietly, for Ruth was a lady
born. When her visit ended I was still faculty waitress.

But I had not counted on Ruth's decisiveness.
After a week or so, I received a letter from her.
I wish I had it by me to quote from now, for nothing
reveals her charm as much as her little notes. It
simply stated that she had got herself a job teaching
physical culture at their local Y.W.C.A., and her
monthly salary was enough to pay my room and
board. Now, she wanted to know, was *that* consecrated enough for me to use—*ma'am?* Not one cent
of her father's money would taint it. "Now, Lamb-
kins, you know it will be good for Ruth to have to
hold down a job! Now don't you? Just think of the
good you are doing me by accepting and thus making me an honest worker in the hive of life, and not
a drone. *Please* write and tell me you accept."

So you see, Ruth had "handled" me after all. I
was never able to handle her, but that is how the
Lord sent me support for the closing school term of
1925.

For Christmas, 1925, I was invited to the Harrison home. Dr. and Mrs. Norman B. Harrison were
now living in St. Louis, where he was pastor of the

famous old Washington-Compton Presbyterian
Church. They have a family of six talented children,
and with two or three of us guests added we made
an hilarious house party. Members of his congregation invited us out to meals and helped to entertain
us, but the most fun were the good times in their
own home, where music and youthful antics embel-
lished every day.

I arrived back at the Institute in January, 1926,
expecting to continue in my luxurious leisure. But a
letter from Ruth was awaiting me. She had taken
sick and the doctor forbade her to continue with her
physical culture class. *"Please* let Father support you
until I get stronger," was her little wail. But I could
not consider it, for it was not the pattern which God
had showed me. One of my lodestar verses was
Hebrews 8:5: "See that thou make all things accord-
ing to the pattern showed to thee in the mount."

From the mountain-top to the valley in one swing.
How often life does just that! One moment having
all things and at the peak of fun, and the next moment facing a grim poverty and hard work. For I
must seek employment now and I had lost the comfortable faculty waitress job—it was never available
for me again. Totally unprepared for this, I had not
been careful in my spending, and now I anxiously
marshaled out my funds. There was just enough to
pay the first month's board—we paid in advance—
with something like eleven or twelve dollars over. I
would barely make it. I must go to the employment
office immediately and see what jobs they could find
for me. The nicer jobs would be all gone by this
time, and more than that, friends had been told that
I was being supported all through school and no one
would think to send me any extra gifts. But the

Lord had not left me. It was another chance to *search* His powers—He was asking me to be willing for uncongenial work again.

As I sat looking at my accounts I suddenly saw something that made me go cold. In the Christmas rush I had forgotten to tithe my last income. What should I do? Let the tithe continue to slide for a while? I pondered a moment. What came first in life anyway? "Oh, Lord, You come first," I whispered and resolutely set aside the tithe. That left me less than two dollars for a month's carfare and incidentals—and I still had no job.

The Institute's Employment Bureau found me two jobs, noon rush-hour girl at the same old restaurant, and waitress for Evening School supper at the Institute. I was now very busy indeed. The long walk to and from the restaurant, and a later hour getting to bed from the evening school began to tell on my health. Always thin, it was dangerous for me to lose weight, but I knew that I was doing so. By February my friends were beginning to notice that I looked haggard and tired, and I myself felt that I was near the breaking point. "Lord, is it Thy will that I have a breakdown?" I prayed in private.

One evening I was called over to the reception room to meet a visitor. Standing there, tall, smiling, and fatherly, was Dr. Harrison. In the city on special speaking engagements, he thought he would look me up. His keen eyes looked searchingly at me as we shook hands and he said, "How is it, Isobel? You look tired. Not working too hard, are you?"

"Perhaps I am," I answered. "When I returned here from your place I found that I must work my way again. The lady who had been supporting me since Marjorie stopped has been sick and cannot do it any more."

"Well, Isobel"—and the keen, kindly eyes again searched my face—"isn't it wonderful that *stop* isn't in the Lord's vocabulary? He never gets sick and He never forgets our needs and He is never at the end of His resources. Do you remember when you were at our place at Christmas that you were invited out to dinner with Marjorie by a Miss Boyle?"

Oh, yes, that had been a real treat. Miss Boyle was a wealthy lady in Dr. Harrison's congregation. She lived in an exclusive apartment hotel, the kind of place where an ordinary mortal scarcely dared to look, much less enter. Because of her love for Marjorie, Miss Boyle had included me in the invitation, but she had scarcely noticed me beyond the usual courteous care of one's guests. But I did not mind that —it left me free to enjoy the exquisite appointments of the room, the table, and the meal. How much the Lord did give me! "As having nothing and yet possessing all things." I was beginning to understand what Paul meant. But Dr. Harrison was talking.

"I saw Miss Boyle just before I left and when she heard me say I was coming to speak at the Institute she said, 'By the way, I was thinking the other day that I have never made any gifts directly to a student at Moody Bible Institute. I feel I would like to help that little friend of Marjorie's who came to my place for lunch that day.' And Isobel, she handed me a check for two hundred dollars. I intended to give it you in small gifts, perhaps ten dollars at a time. But maybe I'd better give it all to you now "

Two hundred dollars—just like that. Truly *at sundry times and in divers manners.*

"Oh, if you did," I cried, "then I could give up one of my jobs and not have to work so hard."

"I'll see you get it morrow, dear," said that dear servant of the Lord, who went on his way.

So I was able to give up the evening work. The noon rush hour, though disagreeable, paid better for the time used, so I retained it. By this and with other gifts I managed to pay my way until summer.

When I returned for the last term (September-December, 1926) I was once more faced with earning my way entirely. The employment bureau put me in touch with Mrs. Frances Allison of the Practical Work Department, who gave me a very special assignment for Sundays—one which paid a salary! I was the Sunday pianist for St. Charles Reformatory for Boys, with the government paying the bill. I gasped at that assignment and expostulated to Mrs. Allison, "Oh, I can't play the piano well enough to hold down that job! I am largely self-taught, and always before, this assignment has been given to a music major student. Isn't that so?"

"True," answered Mrs. Allison, "but I have heard you play for evening devotions, and I think you can make it. I'll ask one of our instructors to give you some tips on evangelistic piano playing and get permission for you to practice on one of the pianos in the music department. The reason I chose you is that this assignment gives such a wonderful opportunity for personal work, and the lady who has been in charge until now is sick. A friend substituting for her is quite inexperienced in bringing children to decisions. You know the Reformatory, don't you? Every kind of boy problem is there, from playing hooky from school to murder. There have been some remarkable conversions and we don't want to

see it slump. You are paid to play for the morning
and afternoon services, but are allowed to visit the
boys who are sick in the infirmary and deal personally with them between services. You get two meals
into the bargain, so it will help you financially."

With fear and trembling I accepted, and for four
months every Sunday brought me thrilling experience. "My strength encampeth on weakness" is one
rendering of II Corinthians 12:9. The substitute
leader who taught the Sunday school lesson in the
morning service was very conscious of her inexperience and the pianist (!) trembled lest she be called
on to give a piano solo, which had sometimes been
done. Truly I was weak, and therefore the Lord
alone was exalted when scores of those boys decided
for Christ. I could fill a chapter with all that took
place at St. Charles Reformatory, but this is a chapter on finances, so I must continue with that theme.

Of course, the salary for piano-playing was only a
mite. I had to take a major job besides that. The
employment office found me another job as a waitress—those hours fitted my schedule best, but at a
select tea-room near Michigan Boulevard. Noon and
evening I was to serve, and the salary promised was
good. It was situated in a private house, and the
clientele were mostly high-salaried clerks or office
workers from the wealthy district around. Undoubt-
edly I would get good tips in addition to the good
salary. The widowed proprietor, Mrs. Mac, had been
investigated, the moral atmosphere of the place had
been approved, and all was trustworthy. Now at last
I ought to have plenty of money, and this was a good
thing, for the last term of school always brings extra
expenses.

I liked it very much. Mrs. Mac was a middle-aged

Southern lady, gracious and warmhearted. The tea-room was pretty, the food delicious, and the clientele very nice to me. My tips grew, and I was congratulating myself when a cloud appeared. At the end of the first month I walked in one morning to hear shouts and high words. The cook was swearing at Mrs. Mac, who was at the telephone.

"Isobel, stay here in this room," commanded Mrs. Mac, all flushed up. "This woman is threatening my life. I've called the police and I do not dare to be left alone with her until they come here and put her out."

"No need for the police if you will give me my salary!" shouted the excited and irate cook. "This is a nice place for you to be in, Miss Isobel! She pays nobody! I've worked here two months and have been paid hardly anything. She owes the butcher, the baker, the—"

"Shut up!" cried Mrs. Mac. "You lie." And then they were at it again when a tall policeman arrived at the door and the cook had to leave.

My heart sank. That wonderful salary—would I really get it? Today was the end of the month and payday. Just what was the situation, anyhow? Within half an hour a new cook had arrived and the business of the day rushed on, but as I went from table to table my mind was busy on this problem. Should I ask Mrs. Mac for my salary? Or should I just pray that God would move her to give it to me? By the end of the day I had made a decision—I would speak if she did not offer to settle accounts. She made no offer, nor did she give any hint that she remembered my salary was due.

"Mrs. Mac," I said as I put on my hat and coat, "tomorrow is the first of the month and I must pay my board and room bill at the Institute. Do you think you could let me have my salary tonight?"

She hesitated, then went slowly over to the till. "I had an unexpectedly big bill to pay today," she said. "Could you take half your salary now and I'll pay you the rest later?"

This was what I had feared. The dismissed cook had told the truth—Mrs. Mac was not in the habit of paying her bills. Her promises were wonderful, but it was quite a different thing to get her to keep them. Again I was in a predicament. If I reported this to the Institute, they would recall me, of course. But at this late date what other jobs would be available? Here at least I received something from tips—in fact, my tips for the first month, combined with what she had just given me, almost equaled the sum of the promised salary, and this gave me an idea.

"Mrs. Mac," I said earnestly, "I am a Christian and accustomed to ask God directly for what I need. I cannot serve you for nothing, but I am willing to keep track of my tips, and at the end of each week if you will make up what is lacking to the amount you promised to pay, I will be content with that. Then we will ask the Lord to move the clients to tip me as much as is needed."

She flushed a little. "But that is not right, Isobel," she said. "The tips should be yours as extra."

"But I am content and can make ends meet if I get what you originally promised me," I replied.

"It is very good of you," she said sadly, then opened up and told me her troubles. I do not believe she was deliberately crooked. She was just utterly undisciplined and improvident, having no conscience about debt, and spent freely what came into the till.

Each Saturday I faithfully reported my tips, which continued to be high. Better able to part with a small sum than a large one, Mrs. Mac gave me her portion. I believe now that I was the only worker she hired who got paid regularly. Of course I talked to her about trusting the Lord for salvation. She liked to listen and often agreed with me, but as far as I could see the miracle of a new birth within her never took place. I fear that the habit of dishonest thinking had become her refuge from conscience. The new cook lasted only six or eight weeks and then there was a scene similar to the first one. She would pay a little on her big butcher's and grocery bills, just enough to keep the stores from suing her, but of course that way of doing business could not go on forever.

One December morning I walked in to find the tea-room empty—nothing cooking in the kitchen, and nothing prepared for the lunch-hour clientele. I called Mrs. Mac, but there was no answer. The upper stories of this beautiful old home had been let out to roomers, and one of them hearing me came downstairs, dressed for departure.

"There has been a big blow-up here," she said in a low voice. "I didn't get it all, but I think the old lady has gone bankrupt. The cook made a furor about salary not paid and Mrs. Mac said she wished she were dead. Do you think she can have hung herself in the cellar? Better go down and have a look! I'm going to my office. Good-by." And I was left alone in the empty room.

There followed a nerve-racking experience. All was silent as the grave, and imagination conjured up my going down a cellar and bumping into her dead body dangling from the rafters. I shook all over and couldn't get up enough courage to open that cellar door. I prayed for the courage to go down and look, but did not receive it. I despised myself and lectured myself and asked the Lord how could I ever go to China if I did not have nerve enough to open a cellar door and go down and investigate. But I was petrified. I just could not do it.

After about an hour at length I heard a step on the veranda and ran forward eager to see another *live* human being. It was Mrs. Mac.

"Oh, Isobel," she said with a heavy sigh, "I forgot about you. There won't be any more tea-room. I'm bankrupt and the receivers are coming to take over the building. I've lost everything. I couldn't stand the silence, so I've been out for a walk."

"Mrs. Mac, I do wish you would give yourself to the Lord!" I said, trying again to help her, but nothing seemed to penetrate her mind. She was appreciative, almost affectionate toward me, but in spiritual matters she was vacant. She would not acknowledge she was a sinner, and that is the first step toward knowing God, so I had to leave her.

Again I was in a predicament—only a few weeks until graduation, and no income! I remember only two details of those last days. Mother had left me her silver service and Father asked to buy it from me for fifty dollars. That helped a lot.

Then came a day when a bill was due and I was five dollars short. I had been praying about it, but nothing had come in. The morning I had to pay it, I received a letter in which five dollars was enclosed, a letter from an old Christian lady whom my father had visited. When he told her I was working my way through Moody, she decided to send me that gift. She had not given me anything before, and she never gave me anything afterward, but on the morning of my lack her five dollars arrived.

At sundry times and in divers manners, always the good hand of my God was upon me. He had wrought wonderfully for Hudson Taylor, but as I looked back over my two years and four months at the Moody Bible Institute I felt He had done just as wonderful things for this little, unknown Bible student. *By searching* I had found God able and faithful to supply my financial needs. And He will do this for any of His children who trust and obey Him.

CHAPTER ELEVEN

GRADUATION AND C.I.M CANDIDATURE

I WAS ELECTED girl class speaker for the graduation exercises in December, 1926. I prayed for a message, taking as my theme, *The Print of the Nails,* based on Thomas's words in John 20:25, "Except I shall see in his hands the print of the nails, and put my finger into the print of the nails, and thrust my hand into his side, I will not believe," making it representative of what the unbelieving world is unconsciously saying to the Christian church today. The heathen around us have not much respect or interest in a smug, ordinary Christianity. "If it costs you nothing, what proof have you that it has any value?" is their indifferent, shrugging attitude. But when they see in any life *the print of the nails,* they are challenged and, like Thomas of old, if they can be made *to see Him* at that moment, they will fall down and cry, "My Lord and my God!"

I felt this message deeply and wanted it to speak to other hearts as it had to my own. The valedictory messages had to be written out, checked for doctrine and grammar, and be memorized by the speakers. This bothered me a little. I didn't mind memorizing the speech, but I had never been able to pour out my heart unless given the freedom of extemporaneous speaking. I did not know this at the time, for I had done comparatively little public speaking. All I knew was that I felt hampered, somehow, on reciting a memorized text. But rules were rules, and I fell in line, as I had tried to do throughout my school days.

My father came to Chicago for my graduation, and Miss Boyle sent me a white silk dress. She and I did not correspond—in fact, apart from the two-hundred-dollar gift at the beginning of that year, I had heard nothing from her. And certainly no one was told that I had no money to buy the required white dress for graduation! (Remember, I had lost my employment at Mrs. Mac's.) Moreover, in those days, Moody Bible Institute required that girl students' clothing have sleeves below the elbow and skirts nine inches from the floor. The 1926 styles were worn shorter than that, yet when Miss Ruby Jackson, Registrar of the Faculty, measured the gift dress, it fulfilled all the requirements and did not have to be altered at all!

Miss Boyle's gifts to me ended here. I have never heard from her since.

As we went up to the platform, on sudden impulse I gave the text of my message to Anne Barr, our vice-president, just in case I got stage fright and needed prompting. I had recited the whole thing more than once before our speech instructor, so it was not that I did not know it.

When my name was called, I went forward and faced that big audience. I did not feel as nervous as I expected to, and started in easily. But as I proceeded, I felt that I was merely reciting and not pouring out my soul. I felt the message was not going into the hearts of the audience and in my anxiety to give it the meaning it had for me, I forgot how the next paragraph started. It was only for a second, however, and Anne behind me prompted quickly in a low voice that not everybody heard, but to me it was a catastrophe. I got through the message, went to my seat, hung my head, and waited until the end of the program when I would be free to dash for my room. Once up there—during my last term I had a room to myself—I fell on my knees in an agony of humiliation and failure Through the heavy city atmosphere a pale December sun shone weakly on me, and then suddenly the Lord was there in the room. I felt His love folding me around. "Never mind, dear," He was saying. "Failure or success, it is all over now, and My love is just the same."

"The beloved of the Lord shall dwell in safety by him; and the Lord shall cover him all the day long, and he shall dwell between his shoulders" (Deut. 33:12).

The words came to me as if spoken, and the tenderness that engulfed me was as the balm of Gilead to my agonized soul. Slowly I quieted, relaxed, rested back on Him, and drank deeply of His love. It was a wonderful experience and I was lifted up in spirit so that I no longer cared about any personal humiliation. I was deeply sorry to have disappointed the expectations of my class, but apart from that *I was beyond hurt.* I have never forgotten the outpouring of God's love upon me that day when I felt such a failure.

After graduation came candidature at the China Inland Mission in Toronto. The 1926 candidates class had been held in August, when Kathryn Kuhn and her brother John, with many others, had been accepted, the party sailing for China in October. I was the only candidate applying in mid-winter, and as I would be leaving for my home on the Pacific coast, the Mission decided that I should come to Toronto immediately after graduation. Toronto being the place of my birth, we had relatives and friends there with whom my father stayed, waiting until he and I could travel west together.

Daddy Page came to the train to see us off. I do not know whether I was looking anxious or sad or just plain tired, but suddenly a tender compassion lit up his face and he leaned forward to say, "Don't be afraid, Isobel. There is nothing to dread in candidate school. The C.I.M. has known you from a child." I thanked him for this good cheer and for all his loving, fatherly care of me during my Institute days, and then the train pulled out.

The Rev. and Mrs. E. A. Brownlee were in charge of the Toronto Mission Home, but Mr. Roy Seaman—the Seamans were on furlough and staying at the Home—was the one appointed to start me on Chinese language study. Candidates learn to recognize the difficult radicals which roughly correspond to the English alphabet, and other simple beginnings. I was also to help and act as companion to the widow of one of the Mission's donors, whose bereavement had made her distraught; her family felt the quiet, prayerful atmosphere of the C.I.M. Home might benefit her.

Dana, son of Mr. and Mrs. Brownlee, was living in the Home, and the only other young person I remember was Miss Ida McInnes. I had met Ida at Moody—indeed, it was she who had organized Daddy Page's surprise birthday party and had intro-

duced me to John—and I had learned to love her.
She had graduated earlier and applied to the China
Inland Mission, but did not pass the medical exam-
ination. China being closed to her, she became office
worker for the Mission to Lepers, but was allowed
to stay on in the C.I.M. Home until she could find
a boardinghouse elsewhere.

Ida was "the embroidery" to my candidate days.
She was devoted to the Lord, and we were one in
the things of the Spirit. Her keen sense of humor was
a safety valve for my youthful spirits. Quick, impulsive, and daydreaming, I had been an easy prey
to *faux pas* all my life and was not in the Home
twenty-four hours before I had made the first one.

Knowing the Brownlees' reputation for perfect
administration I am sure the fault was mine, but I
did not know the daily schedule. Most likely they
had told me while I was daydreaming! Conscious
that this was more than probable, I felt shy to ask
what the hours were, and decided to watch carefully the bells which summoned the household to
meals and meetings. I got along well the first morning, but at half-past one in the afternoon I was
startled by the clang of a bell. What did that call
me to? I rushed to Ida's room, but she was out. A
girl was dusting in the corridor, so I asked her,
"What was the bell for, please?"

She looked at me wonderingly and announced,
"It's the prayer meeting bell."

A prayer meeting? And the candidate not attending? That would look bad!

"Sorry," I said hastily. "I'm new here. Which
room is it?"

She told me, indicating the office buildings, and I
rushed over. The door was shut, but a murmur of

voices within settled it for me. I knocked gently
and opened it. In my excitement, I did not notice
that only the staff was present!

"Excuse me for being late," I murmured and
sank into a seat. They received me politely, albeit
a little blankly, and that day the staff prayers were
very general! After the meeting Mrs. Brownlee came
and told me gently that the half-past one meeting
was for the staff only and that my presence would
not be required.

How Ida laughed when I told her! "They probably *discuss you* at that meeting!" she teased, and
from then on there were many pointed remarks as
to when my presence was required and when it
wasn't. We had hilarious times in her room.

I was in Toronto some three or four weeks before
being called to meet the Council. That is a formi-
dable occasion and I was nervous, as I am not quick
at thinking on my feet. I always do better with
preparation and time to consider the best answer.
The meeting came and went, however, and that
evening after supper I was called into the sitting-
room by Mr. Brownlee to hear the verdict. He said
something like this: "The Council was quite satisfied with your answers today, and we in the Home
have enjoyed your presence. But the Council has
asked me to speak to you upon a very serious matter. Among your referees there was one who did
not recommend you. The reason given was that you
are proud, disobedient, and likely to be a trouble-
maker. This person has known you for some years,
and the Council felt they could not ignore the
criticism."

"Who was it?" I asked quickly, simply dumb-
founded.

"The C.I.M. does 'not betray the confidence of referees. We write to those who have had business associations with you as well as the referees you yourself give—and we promise to keep all reports in confidence. I cannot tell you the name, but I would like to discuss with you what havoc such characteristics can cause on the field."

He then proceeded to do so. At the end of an hour of earnest exhortation, he pronounced the verdict: "The Council decided to accept you conditionally. There is an anti-foreign uprising in China just now which is very serious and we dare not send out any new candidates. That will be our public statement on this matter. For yourself alone, and we hope you will not spread it around, during your waiting period the Vancouver Council will be watching to see if any of these characteristics show themselves. If you prove that you have conquered them, you will then meet with the Western Council and be accepted fully, and sent out with the first party that goes. As we anticipate your victory in these matters, it was voted to pay your train fare to Vancouver, as *en route* for China. I can assure you I have not found it easy to say these things." And indeed his face was sad and tired. I felt sorry for him, even with the misery that was numbing my own heart.

"Good night." And I went up to bed, but, as you can readily believe, not to sleep. Who could be the unknown referee?

Proud. Disobedient. A troublemaker. This was the third time the adjective *proud* had been attached to me. The first time was by Daddy Page himself months before. He had read me an anxious lecture on the subject, to my extreme surprise, for pride

was one of the human frailties of which I felt I was
not guilty. I would have taken Daddy Page's lecture
to heart if he had not ended it by holding up to me,
as one example to emulate, a certain fellow-student.
That particular student stood high in the regard of
the staff, but I happened to room near her and I
knew that secretly she broke many Institute rules,
also she lied about her age to her boyfriends, and
so on. I was sure if Dr. Page knew what I knew, he
would never have held her up as a pattern of conduct. So I concluded he did not know either of us
and brushed the accusation aside. China was later
to be a painful revelation to me of my own heart
and frailty. From this distance I now know that Dr.
Page had indeed sensed a real flaw in my life but
had hold of the wrong label, that was all.

I was selfish. I had whimsically divided the world
into two classes—people who interested me and
people who did not. I felt I was not proud, because
the people who interested me were often among the
poor or the uneducated, but when it was so, my
friendship for them was still as warm as for those
who had social or educational advantages.

Toward people who did not interest me I must
have appeared proud. I cold-shouldered them and
brushed them off me as time-wasters. This was of
course a serious flaw for a missionary, but I fancy
its basis was selfishness rather than pride.

The next point was—disobedience. How I did
get indignant! There were many rules at Moody
Bible Institute which were difficult to keep. The
rules have been revised since, and it is no longer so,
but I had been meticulous in obeying simply because I had signed a promise to do so. I felt honor-
bound to keep that promise. The little matter of

laundry, for instance: we had washbowls in our rooms, but their use for laundry was forbidden. To rinse one pair of stockings a day was allowed, no more. There was no laundry in Ransom Hall, so I had to waste many weary steps going to another dormitory to do my laundry and waste more precious minutes because it was required that each time I get permission from the Matron to do so. And I could not always find the Matron. This was my most galling trial. The girl who had been held up to me as an example washed all her lingerie and sometimes even nightclothes right in her bedroom at hours when she knew the inspectors would be busy elsewhere, and dried them on her radiator! "The rule is unreasonable" was her only answer when I remarked on it. But I had promised to obey, so I dragged my weary self over to the other building every week. And now the C.I.M. had been told I was disobedient!

I had been told not to spread around this second condition of my acceptance by the Mission, but I did write a few friends. They wrote back quickly, indignant and sympathetic, and I was somewhat mollified. All except one, Roy Bancroft, a music student with a beautiful baritone voice and a consecrated heart. We had invited Roy out to St. Charles Reformatory to sing to the boys and help deal with them. I happened to be writing to him those days and impulsively told him. A letter came back quickly and I opened it with a smile of anticipation, thinking that Roy too would be indignant on my behalf.

But I got a shock.

"Isobel," he wrote, "what surprised me most of all was your attitude in this matter. You sound bitter and resentful. Why, if anyone had said to me, 'Roy B., you are proud, disobedient, and a trouble-maker,' I would answer: 'Amen, brother! And even then you haven't said the half of it!' What good thing is there in any of us, anyway? We have victory over these things only as we bring them one by one to the Cross and ask our Lord to crucify it for us."

These words "stabbed my spirit broad awake." Faithful friend he was, not afraid to season his words with salt even as he did not forget to speak with grace also. I was on my knees in no time asking the Lord to forgive me.

I arose from my knees with a different attitude. Instead of resentment there was alertness to watch and see if these three horrid "Diabolutians"—pride, disobedience, rebellion—were really lurking in my camp The town of Mansoul should not protect them, if detected. This brought me into peace, even though I always shrank from the memory that I was to be watched for their appearance in my life.

Subsequently it so happened that in a most unexpected way I learned of my detractor's identity and then I knew the reason for her hostility. It will suffice here to say that she was a teacher in a school which I had attended. She wished me to assist her in spying on my fellow-pupils. I felt that was unworthy and so had incurred her displeasure by refusing. When I learned this I was tempted to clear myself with Mr. Brownlee and the Western Council. But should I? I seemed to hear a voice say, "If that had been said of me, I'd have answered 'Amen, Brother! And then you haven't told the half of it!' " Dear old Roy—he was right. Why try to make the Mission think I was lily-white? They'd have per-

sonal experience before long as to just how earthly
a person I was!

"No, Lord!" I whispered. "I won't bother the
Mission with it. But how princely ot You to let me
know—it is like a miracle. Only You could have
done it."

> For the Lord is always kind;
> Be not blind.

Kind? To let me end up at Moody, where I had
striven so to be faithful, under such a cloud? To let
me begin with the C.I.M. under such a stigma?
Kind?

Yes. You see, the Lord foreknew there was a
work to be done in Vancouver before I sailed for
China, and if I had ended up Institute life with
great *éclat* I would quite possibly have wrecked that
work at the very outset. My self-confidence needed
to be thoroughly jarred before He dare put this delicate affair into my hands. And He jarred it all right.
My Master is thorough, and "no one worketh like
Him." But He had also been meticulously kind—
just as soon as He dared, He showed me why. And
that after-graduation ceremony experience of His
enfolding love has blessed me all my life.

Only *by searching* can we find out what He is.

Again to jump ahead of my story, but to complete
this little matter, when the door did open for China
again Mr. Thomson wrote me a letter. I cannot quote
it verbatim, but it ran like this: "I have never mentioned to you that little condition of the Toronto
Council. From the first, both Professor Ellis and I
felt there was a mistake somewhere, and I want you
to know that so thorough was our confidence in this
that I have not felt it even necessary to call the

Western Council together. I telephoned each one of them, and we all want you to know that you are accepted by the China Inland Mission unconditionally and unanimously. Every one of them said that. And our loving prayers and blessings go with you."

I bowed my head over that little letter and wept tears of gratitude. Yes, my Master is thorough. He wounds, but He binds up, and His balm of Gilead heals without stinging; it cools, refreshes, and restores in every part. He gives the garment of praise for the spirit of heaviness, and brings beauty out of our ashes.

CHAPTER TWELVE

THE VANCOUVER GIRLS
CORNER CLUB

FATHER AND I TRAVELED on the train together from Toronto to Vancouver, where my brother Murray met us at the station. It was strange to be together without Mother, and still more strange to find myself going across the ferry to North Vancouver in order to get *home*.

Father and Murray had rented a small four-room bungalow on Twelfth Avenue. Dad had one bedroom, I was given the other, and Murray put up a cot in the sitting room at night and slept there. The fourth room was a kitchen. A bathroom separated the two small bedrooms, and a good big basement took in my trunk and suitcases. The little place was scarcely big enough for the three of us. There were familiar things in the house—Mother's piano, the well-known parlor chairs, friendly bookcases, and a big fireplace—just like the one in the old home. It was good to be back and I came to love that little house on the hill. From the front porch I could see the harbor and the waters of Burrard Inlet, beyond which lay—China.

There now faced me the need for employment. I must earn my living until the door to China re-

opened. Was I to go back to schoolteaching? I
would have to sign a contract and then would not
be free to leave if the way opened before the contract expired. I felt great reluctance in spirit to do
this. God had led me *out* of schoolteaching. I felt it
would be like sending Abraham back to Ur of the
Chaldees to return to it. While I was praying and
pondering I received an invitation to speak to the
Vancouver Girls Corner Club (V.G.C.C.) at their
evangelistic service on the next Tuesday night. Yes,
I replied, I would be very pleased to be their
speaker. Then, hanging up the phone, I asked my
father who the V.G.C.C. were.

"Christian business girls banded together to try
to win other business girls to the Lord," answered
Father. "The Club was founded by Mrs. Neff, a
worker in the big evangelistic campaign held here
when you were in your teens. Don't you remember?
Well, when the meetings were over they had a final
supper with the converts, and some of the business
girls got into a corner to discuss how they could
keep together and keep going on after the campaign
ended. They decided to form a club and to hold a
weekly meeting to bring in unsaved friends. 'Here
we are in a corner,' said one jokingly. 'Let's call it
the *Corner Club*.' And that is how it started and
how it got its name. It is a fine work and I am glad
you are going to speak to them."

The next Tuesday evening Father took me downtown to the Club rooms. They had a big lounge
overlooking Granville Street, one of the busiest
streets of the city, a small office for their Superintendent, and a big dining hall where we went for
supper. On Tuesday evenings a good supper was
furnished for only fifteen cents a person. The des-

sert was always cake, and those delicious cakes were baked and donated by the women's societies in various churches, thus enabling the supper price to be kept low.

After supper the tables were cleared, pushed back, and the chairs arranged for the meeting. A platform and piano were at the end of the long room and a bright evangelistic service was conducted for an hour. Christian business girls themselves led this meeting, and it was an enjoyable time, I thought.

In less than a week I received a second phone call. It was from the girls' President of the V.G.C.C., who astounded me by an invitation to become their Superintendent! I had not noticed that the position was vacant, but apparently they had been without one for some time. "We feel shy to ask you to take it," said the President, "because we can't afford to pay you the salary you deserve, or even as much as we have paid in the past. Corner Club is run down a bit, having gone so long without a Superintendent. We can give you only eighty dollars a month to start with, but as the work picks up we hope to increase it. Your hours will not be heavy, and you will not need to be in the office until ten o'clock each morning."

When I asked what were the duties of the Superintendent, she replied, "Well, to lead and direct the work. Every day at noon, tea, coffee, and milk are sold in the dining room. Business girls bring their bag lunches there and enjoy getting hot drinks to go with them. You will circulate among these girls, get to know them, and try to lead them to the Lord. Every Tuesday evening you will be in charge of the evangelistic service and will speak. The Corner Club has had to draw speakers from various churches in the city during this period without a Superintendent, and we would like to pay back our debt to them, so to speak, by having you speak at any of their young people's societies who invite you. This would also advertise the Club. And maybe you yourself will create some new activities. Remember our motto is *The Other Girl*."

I asked for time to pray about it and a date was set for my answer.

Nothing else was offered to me, and as I waited in prayer I felt the Lord wanted me to accept this invitation. So it came about that I became Superintendent of the Vancouver Girls Corner Club for 1927 and part of 1928. I had stipulated that the moment the door to China opened, I should be free to resign, and that was agreed to.

I now entered upon a fascinating period of my life. Corner Club was run by a Girls' Board, a Women's Board—representatives from different churches and denominations in the city—the Superintendent, and a business manager.

The business manager was a godly, middle-aged woman whom everyone called Mother Fitch. Mrs. Fitch was one of those energetic saints who are described as being *full of good works*. She had not enjoyed a higher education but had been taught of the Spirit and lived for the glory of God and the winning of souls. There was no big evangelistic effort in Vancouver without Mother Fitch having a hand in it somewhere. The city missions were enriched by her prayers and practical services. Realizing that God had not trained her for platform work, she humbly accepted any mundane service—cooking, serving, or even scrubbing—and prayed it into a ministry of blessing. Every Sunday she went to the jails to preach and during the week she ran the kitchen department of the Corner Club. Needless to say, I found in her a kindred spirit, although she must have been more than twice my age. We were a queer-looking team, but always a united one.

The Girls' Board were elected by members of the Club. I was only twenty-five years old by now, and most of the Girls' Board, I think, would have been a bit older than that, but our times together are among my happiest memories. I have always felt that my Corner Club girls were among the loveliest young women that God ever made. They were ready for any venture that would win souls, but they were also a very merry group, and the Club rooms resounded with laughter and gay banter in between the earnest prayer meetings and discussions.

I did not meet the Women's Board immediately, and Mother Fitch laid hold of me early in that first week with a warning.

"Isobel," she said, "I would like to suggest to you that you do away with the Women's Board. They are not spiritually minded like the Girls' Board, and I think they may be a drag on you. I believe God has sent you here for a red-hot soul-winning campaign and I am behind you one hundred per cent. You preach and I will cook! I know my place. The Women's Board won't allow you to give a call to decision on Tuesday nights, and I'm afraid you will meet with other restrictions. It is true the Club does get support from their churches and they would cut it off if the Women's Board were dissolved, but I am willing to live by faith like Hudson Taylor, and I am sure you are too. I think you could talk the girls into agreeing, for they are anxious to give you a free hand to direct things as God leads you."

Now this was the delicate situation into which I had come. I was young, inexperienced, and the words *red-hot soul-winning campaign* thrilled my soul. To give up a salary and live like Hudson Taylor would be heroic—the strongest kind of appeal to me at that time. It was many years before a quiet article in the C.I.M.'s private *News Bulletin* alerted me to the danger of *missionary heroics*. The article pointed out that just because a line of action is difficult, painful, or dangerous does not necessarily prove that it is the will of God. A simple illustration was cited: A call for medicine comes in the middle of a missionary's meal. She jumps up and leaves her food half eaten and rushes off to answer. That may seem noble and sacrificial on the surface, but in reality it could be foolish and harmful. Of course, I am not referring to life-and-death emergencies, when promptness is a duty. I mean an ordinary medical call. The messenger has probably dilly-dallied several times already and an extra ten minutes' wait until the nurse's needed nourishment is properly masticated will hurt no one. As I read the article, I recognized my own behavior pattern with deep chagrin. I was not given to breaking up my mealtimes, but I had been guilty of other extremes of conduct. Some natures are more open to this temptation than others, and mine is one. So at this time of my youth, Mother Fitch's suggestion appealed to me as quite possibly the highest line of conduct. I was cautious, however, and told her we must pray much before doing anything so radical.

I believe it was that very evening when I met the President of the Women's Board. She was a warm-

hearted Scottish lady who shook hands with me, giving me a hearty welcome to the Corner Club. Then
she added: "You are a candidate of the C.I.M.,
aren't you? I'm good friends of Mr. and Mrs. Charles
Thomson, and he told me to keep an eye on you
and let him know *how you get on here!*" And she
beamed at me cordially, perfectly unconscious that
she had just brought a whiplash down over my
shoulders with a sting!

I never for a moment thought that Mr. Thomson
had betrayed our secret to her. Charles Thomson
was a godly Scotsman, the soul of honor and common sense. I was sure that Mrs. Mc—— did not
know the full implication of what she had said, but
I saw in a second that I was in no position to begin
my Superintendent's career by dismissing her! Some
more gentle method must be found, so the Lord
used this whiplash to guide me on to a better road.
I told Mrs. Fitch that I felt we should go slowly and
try what prayer could do first. She sighed, but never
refused a challenge to pray. The day was to come
when the President of the Women's Board would
kneel beside me in the little office, and with tears
thank God that He had brought me to Corner Club.
And I—likewise with tears in my heart—thanked
Him for keeping me from the precipitate action
which would have wounded this dear life and hin-
dered the accomplishment of His purposes.

As I gradually met with other members of the
Women's Board I found a group of women very
different in temperament one from the other, but
gifted, reasonable, and co-operative. They did ask
that I issue no calls to come forward for decision,
feeling that the business girls would prefer more
decorum and dignity in the Tuesday night services

than the usual penitent form method, but they too
wanted to see people converted.

God blessed the Tuesday night meetings in a quiet
way. Not many made an open profession of Christ
(which troubled me) but the attendance grew by
leaps and bounds. No one knew how difficult I
found those services. I was tormented by fear of
stage fright again, or my mind going blank like it
had during the M.B.I. graduation ceremony. Many
a Tuesday night, as the girls were gaily putting out
the hymnbooks, I slipped down the corridor to the
bathroom—the only place where I could be sure not
to be seen—and, leaning up against the wall, cried
to the Lord for nerve to go back and get on that
platform. He never failed me: the stage fright never
came back seriously, and gradually I began to
count on His help, and speaking grew easier.

Invitations to churches began to come, too. Finding that several of the girls had beautiful voices, I
organized and trained a quartet, following the teaching I had received at Bible school in this. One of the
younger members of the Women's Board had a bell-
like contralto voice suited to sing the bass part, so
the quartet represented both the Girls' and Women's
Boards and was a real success. "Miss Miller and the
Corner Club Quartet" began to get calls from all
different denominations, and our opportunities to
witness for the Lord multiplied. Often we took our
suppers to the Club and ate before leaving as a
team for the church of the evening. Then it was that
the empty dining-room rang with laughter, for all
four had a keen sense of humor and the relaxation
from their office work prompted an ebullition of
youthful spirits. But always the evening's work was

brought before the Lord in earnest petition before we left.

I began to see what a power a Christian Business Girls' Club could be. Through its interdenominational character, it was quietly reaching out and challenging young people's societies in many denominations throughout the city.

And even into the business life of the city an influence was going out. A lawyer asked what had caused the change in the life of his stenographer and her answer had an effect on him. I saw more and more the wonderful potentialities of the work when first things were kept first. There have been corner clubs in other cities, but the temptation is to let them sink into merely social service efforts. Young life must have an outlet, and I soon saw that. So we had picnics, seaside corn roasts, hikes on Saturday afternoon, and in the winter we had a stunt night for girls only. This was one of the most hilarious evenings I ever spent. The stunts were all wholesome fun and revealed much brains and talent. I myself had opened it, dressed up as a cartoon version of an old maid schoolmarm, and I announced that the students of my boarding school were about to put on a program for their relatives and friends. Most of the girls had never seen me lay aside the dignity of my office just for fun, and it tickled their fancy to find I could enjoy a joke as much as the next one. That stunt night broke the ice between me and a certain girl for whom I had been fishing in vain for several weeks. It was only a short time afterward that she accepted the Lord in my office. But all our parties were threaded through with the love of Him, and a deadly earnestness that others might find Him too. I think that is the secret. A merely social club helps nobody very much, for it does not offer any solution to the problems of life.

My noontime circulating among the lunchers was to me the most difficult part of my work. Always shy about meeting strangers, I also had this unfortunate background of having so fiercely resented personal work in my own earlier days that it made me timid to barge in on other lives. I always felt I was a failure in those noon contacts, where a gifted evangelist could no doubt have reaped a big harvest. But I made friends and had their confidence. The sins and temptations which they gradually opened up to me about were appalling and led us into many unexpected adventures.

Let me tell about two of them.

Edith was a clever young girl who had come out from England to get work in Canada, and she lived with an aunt while doing so. She met and fell in love with a young man, and we followed her joy through the day she appeared in the lunch room with her new diamond ring, to the time when she said good-by to office work and invited us all to her wedding. She had her dress and trousseau, had resigned her job, the wedding day was set, and the invitations had all been mailed. A night or so before the wedding her telephone rang. Edith heard a strange woman's voice on the wire: "Is it true that you are to be married to Mr. So-and-so in a couple of days?"

"Yes," answered Edith, wonderingly.

"I am very sorry, but I must tell you he is already married. I am his wife. I have our wedding certificate here."

Can you imagine the shock of this to that young English girl? The shame of it? The heartbreak—for she had given her love unreservedly? But you cannot imagine the worst. Her aunt, humiliated at having to cancel the wedding, in a towering rage ordered the girl out of the house. She would have no such thing of shame under her roof, she said.

Out on the street, homeless, wild with grief and heartache, where could Edith go? Her church? They were her aunt's type and would probably hold the same views. *Corner Club.* She crept in, broken, distraught—then found herself clasped on Mother Fitch's broad bosom. Corner Club protected her, loved her, found her a home, and led her to the Lord. She proved to be an exceptionally gifted girl, and it was only a year or two before she had earned enough money to go back to England, where her own mother still lived. It was a soul saved and a young life saved as well.

The most exciting story perhaps was that of Flossie. A knock on my office door came one afternoon and I opened it to see a fashionably dressed woman standing there.

"Miss Miller?" she asked. "May I have a word with you? I have been to your Club rooms several times and admire the work you are doing very much. There is a young girl named Flossie in my boardinghouse who needs help. May I tell you about her?"

I led the woman into the lounge and we sat while she talked. "Flossie is a nice young thing from the prairies. Her mother is a widow, I believe, who sent her to Vancouver to study to be a nurse. She is a pretty girl and seems to have a lot of dates with young doctors, you know, and I guess she neglected her studies. Anyway, she failed her year, is out of the hospital, and has no money. I am anxious that

the temptations of a big city do not suck her under.
Do you think your Corner Club could help her?
I told her you were very nice, despite—ahem—
your long hair, and—ahem—your long skirts"—this
with an eye to each. (The fashions in 1927, you
remember, had shrunk skirts until they barely
reached the knees, and although I had shortened
my dresses I still felt that modesty required that the
knees be covered. My hair should be long for the
China of those days, so I had never cut it.)

I was much amused at her two "ahems," but
boldly ignored this little difference of opinion between us, and answered, "We will certainly do anything we can to help Flossie. We are not an employment agency, but—"

"But do you have dishes to wash and dry?" urged
the lady. "I thought if you could employ her here
it would give you a chance to talk to her and perhaps steady her."

"I will consult our business manager," I replied.
"Leave me your telephone number and I will call
you. We do have dishes to wash, but our help is
voluntary. Our budget does not allow for much
paid labor."

Mother Fitch, of course, was enthusiastic about
taking in another young life to influence for Christ,
and it was agreed to employ her for a week or so
while we sought to get her regular employment. So
Flossie was brought to us.

She turned out to be a gay little chatterbox. Most
of the time she was busy in the kitchen, of course,
but there came an hour when I was able to have her
alone in the office and presented the claims of the
Lord Jesus for her heart and life. She listened with
the tears running down her face and acquiesced in

everything. When she had left, Mother Fitch came
in to inquire about the result.

"Well," I answered slowly, "I am not satisfied.
She was certainly touched and willing to follow me
in prayer and accept Christ as her Saviour. She
wept, but somehow I cannot believe she is born
again. Something did not seem to click—if you
know what *i* mean."

Although we were not an employment agency,
and certainly not a rescue mission, still it was possible at Corner Club to announce to the girls that
a certain one needed work and to ask that the members keep their eyes open for a suitable vacancy.
This we did, and Flossie was not with us long
before a noon-hour girl named Helen came to my
office.

"Do you suppose, Isobel," she said, "that this girl
Flossie would be willing to take a poorly paid job
until something better turns up? My mother has
had a stroke and is completely paralyzed—she cannot even turn in bed. I am only an office worker
and cannot afford a trained nurse to care for her
during the day while I am away. But Flossie has
had some training. I would give her room and board
and a little pocket money if she would come and
care for Mother."

We called Flossie in, and she accepted the position. She would be free every evening and we urged
her to come to our Tuesday supper and service, and
said good-by. As our life was full of unexpected
cases, it was not possible to follow up Flossie very
closely.

Summer came, and I was to have two weeks'
vacation, which I chose to spend at The Firs, natu-

rally. A few days before I was to leave I had a telephone call from Helen.

"Isobel, have you heard about Flossie?" she asked.

"No, not a word," said I in alarm. "Please tell me."

"Well, she is in the hospital. She began to act and talk strangely here and one evening she had a sort of spell so I called in a doctor. He sent her to her old hospital and now says she is insane. I don't believe it myself. In fact, I think she is acting a part to get away from here. It is a bit quiet for her, I guess. I feel she's been accustomed to hit the pace, you know. Anyway, I wish you would go and see her. Her doctor might believe you. He won't listen to me. Here is his name and telephone number."

I was staggered at this news, but promised to go and see Flossie. Helen hung up and I called the doctor's number. A crisp, professional voice answered.

"Doctor, this is Miss Miller, Superintendent of the Vancouver Girls Corner Club. I believe you are treating Flossie ———?"

"Yes," he said, shortly.

"Well, our Club is interested in her, and I have been asked to go and see her at the hospital if you will allow it."

"It would do no good, Miss Miller," came the answer quickly. "She would not know you. She recognizes no one and I have had her put in the violent ward."

"Well, Doctor, the friends with whom she was staying feel that she is just acting a part."

An exclamation of anger stopped me. "Miss Miller, I have been a specialist in mental cases for many years. Do you presume to tell me I cannot recognize insanity?" He was clearly insulted.

"No, Doctor. I beg your pardon. But for the sake of her friends, could you not give me permission to visit Flossie? My pronouncement would quiet them."

He gave an exclamation of impatience.

"All right. Be at the hospital on Saturday afternoon at two. I'll give orders for you to be admitted." He slammed down the receiver.

Down went my phone, too. And up went my heart to the Lord. "Now, O Lord, I'm in for it! I have a new search on now. Can you control the highstrung bunch of nerves which is me, and enable me to face an insane person?"

I think that most people must have a private horror, a phobia, about some one thing. Most women fear snakes. I've known a big man almost to go to pieces at the news that a rat was near. A famous scholar of our generation admits to a phobia regarding insects. Now my own private fear has always been insanity. I don't like snakes or rats, but they do not set my nerves ajingle like the word *insane*.

"Lord," I prayed, "when I felt I should go down into that cellar to see if Mrs. Mac had hung herself there, I asked You for the nerve to go, *and I didn't get it*. Of course, You knew she wasn't there and that I didn't need to look. But still—can You nerve me to face insanity? Saturday afternoon will be my proving time."

I was to leave on Saturday night for The Firs, so I was packed and ready for the train. Leaving my baggage at the Corner Club, I proceeded to the hospital at two o'clock in the afternoon and inquired for the ward where Flossie was. It was in the basement.

Across the corridor were heavy, locked doors, and in front of them, at the side was a desk with two nurses in attendance. On the other side of the doors, someone was singing a ragtime song at the top of her lungs.

I went up to the nurses and said, "Please, may I see Flossie ———?"

The nurses looked at one another. "I'm sorry," said the elder of the two. "It's against the rules. No one is allowed to see her."

"But I was told that I might, if I came at this hour," I said. Again they exchanged glances, then the younger nurse said to me, "She is violent. That is her singing now." The youthful voice was rollicking on.

"Dr. ——— told me he would give orders to let me in," I protested. That was a magic word. "Oh," they said, scrambling through some papers on the desk. "Yes, here is an order for a Miss Miller."

"I am Miss Miller."

"All right. Step this way."

The nurse took a big bunch of keys and opened the corridor door, ushering me into the aisle on the other side. Small cells lined this corridor on both sides, and each door was locked. The cells were beneath ground level, but had one iron-barred window high up near the ceiling, level with the ground outside.

My heart was beating so violently I felt dizzy and sick, but before I knew what was going to happen, the nurse had unlocked a cell, and pushed me in alone. I heard her lock the door behind me!

Flossie stood with her back to the door, looking up through the little barred window and shouting her song. She was in a disheveled mess that it would

not be kindness to describe. At the sound of the
key in the door she whirled around like a wild animal about to spring on its prey, but as soon as she
saw me she went limp, blinked stupidly for a moment, then said, "Miss Miller!"

"Yes, Flossie dear," I answered. Going forward
and taking her in my arms, I kissed her. "I've only
just learned that you were sick. I've come to see
you. Get into bed, dear, and then we can talk."

Like a lamb she climbed on to her cot and I sat
at the foot of it, as there was no chair in the cell—
nothing else but the iron bed. I talked about the
Corner Club, trying to draw her memory back to
quiet things and to the Lord. She answered each
question intelligently and only once did she exhibit
anything strange. I was telling her of some little
Corner Club incident and said, "Mother Fitch—
you remember who she is, Flossie, don't you?"

"Yes," came from the young face on the pillow.
Then there followed an expression of cunning, *"And
I know you,"* she cried emphatically. I went cold
all down my spine, but ignored it, continuing my
quiet chit-chat. I told her to trust in the Lord and
promised to write her mother. "I am going on my
vacation," I said, "but will come and see you as soon
as I get back." I stayed about fifteen minutes, then
knocked loudly on the door, hoping the nurse would
hear. She came at length and I left—leaving Flossie
still lying quietly in bed.

When I got back to the Corner Club I telephoned
the doctor. "Yes," he said. "Well, how did you
get on?"

"She knew me immediately, Doctor, and called
me by name."

There was a staggered silence at the other end

of the line, then I heard him say to himself, "Well I'll be——." To me he said, "Miss Miller, please tell me exactly what happened, right from the first." After I had done so, he said, "How soon can you visit her again?"

"I am leaving in a few hours for vacation, Doctor. I will be gone two weeks, but will call you as soon as I return."

"You do that!" he said earnestly, and we hung up.

Of course, I felt that Helen must be right—Flossie was playing a part for some reason. If I had known it was so important, I would have given up my vacation to attend her, but I didn't. In my next telephone conversation with the doctor on my return from The Firs he told me she had been sent to an insane asylum outside Vancouver. He was quite indifferent whether I visited her or not, saying, "This time she won't know you," but he gave me permission for a visit with her.

Looking back at this incident after nearly thirty years, and after having had more than two decades of experience with devil-worshiping mountain tribes, I am inclined to think that Flossie was demon-possessed. The Devil has hoodwinked educated America into thinking he is a myth, and he is working havoc unrecognized. My reason for believing this is twofold. First, I found that *the mere presence* of a consecrated Christian in a demon-haunted house was enough to force back those powers. My entrance into that hospital cell brought with it the power of my Master and the demon force was temporarily quelled. Second, that look of cunning when she affirmed—unasked!—that she knew me, was the very same that I have seen on the face of a demon-possessed tribes girl just before that demon was cast out. And the compulsion to confess recognition is similar to what took place in our Lord's day. But as Superintendent of the Corner Club, I knew as yet nothing of these matters.

Now I felt I must visit Flossie in the asylum. Again I was terrified at the thought, but as God had taken care of me in the hospital, He would surely help me in this second step. So one afternoon found me arriving by bus at the famous institution which I had never dreamed I would ever see.

It was a huge place several stories high, and as I approached the large entrance, men patients behind the iron bars of a veranda screamed out to me and thrust their arms through the bars as if trying to reach me. Not very soothing to the nerves! Inside, I was ushered first into the office of the resident physician. He was a young man, and as I advanced to his desk he exclaimed, "Why, it is Miss Miller!" It was my turn to be astonished.

"Isobel Miller of Arts 22, U.B.C. (University of British Columbia), isn't it?" he repeated, shaking hands cordially.

"Why, yes. But how do you know?" I queried. He laughed.

"I was an undergraduate, a year or so behind you. What have you been doing since then?"

We had a little chat. My work at the Corner Club brought up the name of Flossie. There must have been several thousand patients in that place, so I asked, "Would you possibly know Flossie?"

"Would I?" he returned. "I'll never forget the night they brought her here. It took four strong men to hold her!"

"What do you think? Is she incurable?"

"No-o," he answered thoughtfully. "This type is

brought on by dissipation and with the use of modern drugs we can often effect a cure. Did she talk very much? That is the first sign of this condition coming on—extreme talkativeness. She'll be here two years at least, though, and then there is likely to be a recurrence later on."

"My Club would like to help. Of course, we believe that prayer will help her, but is there anything else you can suggest?"

"Yes," he answered. "She is run down through late hours and the life she led. If your Club can send her nourishing food, with extra protein values, such as meats and broths, that might hasten her recovery. The ordinary food here is good, but she needs extra meat and such, which a government institution can hardly provide."

I promised that we would do our best, and he rang for an orderly to show me the way to Flossie's ward.

"They must prepare her to see you," he warned, "so you will have to wait awhile."

Again I was taken to a corridor with a locked door. A lounge opened off at the side where harmless patients were sitting around, some embroidering, some reading, one playing the piano, and a nurse at a desk was obviously in charge. I sat in a bench opposite the locked door. Up tripped a young woman who asked me boldly, "Who have you come to see?"

"Flossie ——," I replied, rather wonderingly.

"Oh yes, a nice girl, I know her!" This with a loud voice, her eyes on the matron at the desk. Then behind her hand in a whisper she said to me, "She is no more insane than I am."

"I've brought her some chocolates. Do you think

she'll like them?" I asked, more to make conversation than anything else.

"Oh, yes. The food here is fine!" This also in a loud voice toward the Matron, then behind her hand in a whisper, "It's awful. They starve us. Bring her *lots* of chocolates!" And so she went on— compliments in a loud voice for the Matron to hear, and complaints in a whisper behind her hand to me. It was all I could do to keep my face straight, but evidently she was known to them, for after a few minutes the Matron quietly lifted her head and ordered, "K——, you come back in here."

"See our bondage!" whispered the woman, making a wry face to me—but she obeyed.

At length a nurse came with a key and I was again ushered in behind the door to where a second nurse had brought Flossie, then to my horror both nurses left me alone and locked me in with the patient.

I would not have recognized Flossie. She was so thin and a mere shadow of herself. The preparation they had given her was to drug her into stupidity, then immerse her, hair and all, in a bath to clean her up. She stood before me swaying unsteadily, her damp hair clinging to her like a drowned rat, and she obviously did not know me. I told her my name and repeated it, but she gave no sign of recognition. I proffered the chocolates and she opened them eagerly, popping them into her mouth one after the other rapaciously. Within five minutes I knew that conversation was useless. It was true, she did not know me nor could she follow my thoughts.

Then the effect of the drug began to wear off

She had been brought to me in a corridor, with rooms on both sides.

"I want to go back!" she said suddenly, and started staggering down the corridor, hunting for her own room. As I did not know which one it was, I knocked and banged on the locked door to call the nurses back. At length one of them came and took Flossie to her place. But by this time Flossie had evidently come to. She turned fiercely on the nurse, swore, and cursed her. A glimpse into the room showed me why they had to drug her and bathe her before allowing any other human being to see her. Obviously she was living like an animal. Heartsick, I turned away and came home. It was an experience I would not care to have often, but the Lord had strengthened me to go through with it.

At the Corner Club I did not describe what I had seen, but merely gave the doctor's advice to send her nourishing foods. I told how emaciated she was and asked for prayer. I also wrote to her mother and the result was that a sister was sent to Vancouver to visit Flossie and care for her needs.

Prayer was made constantly for the poor child's recovery, and cartons of jellied chicken, home-made broths, jellies, and other good foods were sent by the girls and the Women's Board. Still we were not prepared for our dear Lord's answer to our prayers, abundantly above all that we had asked or thought.

Within six months Flossie was dismissed, cured. After asking the Lord daily to do this, I was taken aback by the speed with which His answer came. One day I received a telephone call from a stranger which ran something like this: "Miss Miller, you do not know me, but I am Mrs. ——, neighbor of Flossie's mother on the prairies. My husband an

I are on a trip to the coast and Flossie's mother asked me to bring Flossie home with me when we return. Do you know she was dismissed from the hospital a few days ago? No? Well, she was. She is living with her sister, but would like to come and see you before she leaves and thank you for what you have done for her. May I bring her this afternoon? We leave by the evening train. Thank you. At three o'clock, then."

I sat back in my swivel chair and gasped. Then I bowed my head and thanked the Lord.

I awaited three o'clock with a little trepidation. I had met two very different Flossies already. Which one would this one resemble? The gay chatterbox? The doped animal? Could she really be normal? The third Flossie was the real Flossie, and a distinctly different person still. She had gained weight to a pleasing plumpness, but was so shy and quiet I could hardly recognize her. She thanked me prettily and sincerely, but when she was gone into the kitchen to salute Mother Fitch I turned to their neighbor and said, "My, she is quiet! Do you think she is afraid of me?"

The lady widened her eyes with astonishment. "Oh, no. Flossie never did talk much. She was always the quiet one. She is just like she used to be. Her mother will be delighted."

And so we parted. But my story isn't ended.

Nine years passed and now I was back at the Corner Club as a missionary on furlough, a married woman and a mother. What a welcome they gave me! But before the first message, which they asked me to give at the old Tuesday evening hour, I had a telephone call.

"Isobel, I wonder if you will remember me. This is Flossie."

I nearly jumped out of my skin. "Flossie! You back in Vancouver?"

"Yes. But I'm married now. Oh, Isobel, the Lord has been so good to me. I want to tell you all about it before you meet my husband. Will you take supper with me downtown, just the two of us alone, and then I will go with you to the meeting? My husband is coming to the meeting tonight—I got permission to bring him, since John, another man, will also be present. But I want you to hear my story first."

I wonder if you can understand my joy? No one can who has not mothered spiritual children. No one can who has not stood and watched the brand blazing in the fire, and then shrunk from the heat which almost scorched the hand stretched out to snatch it from the burning!

That evening in a little cubbyhole of a restaurant we sat face to face once more. She was still sweet-faced Flossie, her quiet manner lit up with heartfelt gratitude. "Yes, I have a good husband and two darling children. *And I've never had a recurrence.* I'm sure the Lord won't let me now. And, Isobel, I want my children to be brought up in the church. My husband and I are agreed: we want a Christian home."

Just one little peach from a year's harvest at the Corner Club. What potentialities lie in such work—leading business girls to Christ!

Often, on furloughs, I have heard the impatient remark, "Why go to the foreign field? There is lots to be done at home here!" There most certainly is.

And there are lots of Christians at home—but are they doing it?

By searching for Him, He makes us conscious of the need of others, and helps us cut channels by which He may be poured into their lives. In no time we find ourselves His fellow workers, and life is rich.

But I must come back to my tale: for by now the door to China was opening again.

CHAPTER THIRTEEN

"LET US GO ON!"

It was the spring of 1928 when the China Director of the China Inland Mission, the Rev. George Gibb, paid a visit to Vancouver. I was called in to meet him and well remember the searching look of concern he gave me. "My dear girl," he said, "you look worn out. Are you well enough to go to China?"

"Oh, yes. Physically I am sound. But I am very tired," I admitted. Our home on the north side was so far away from the evening church appointments. Late at night the ferry did not run so frequently, and if I missed one there was a long wait before the next. Often it was midnight before I got to bed, and six o'clock was my rising hour if I was to have a quiet time, get the house chores done, and catch the nine o'clock ferry.

But I think most of it was emotional fatigue. Mentally I knew the way of victory. I had read of Hudson Taylor's experience, *The Exchanged Life,* when he rolled all his burdens on the Lord. I had heard Keswick teaching expounded at The Firs and had seen it lived in lives there. But how to transmute it into experience was beyond me. I secretly worried about things. My father's Micaw-

ber-like attitude toward business appalled me. Where
would he end up? Now I knew what my mother's
secret trial had been and how much we all owed to
her sound judgment and carefulness.

I worried about my own failure at the Corner
Club. I did not have the gift of evangelism. Young
lives were constantly being cleansed, rededicated
and built up in Him, but I did not see that. I looked
just for souls to take the initial step of salvation.
Pentecostal girls were urging me to seek the baptism of the Spirit. One of them was a gifted evangelist, a golden-haired, angel-faced girl, and I fell into
the snare of comparing myself with others. Peggy
had something I didn't. Was it really the speaking
in tongues? Inwardly I fretted. But the Lord was
carefully holding me. I asked Peggy and Dorothy—
another girl who kept at me—to describe what happened when they were "filled with the Spirit." Their
most vivid descriptions were no more than what I
myself had often experienced when alone with the
Lord and the awareness of His presence would flood
in. I had never spoken in tongues, but I seemed to
have had everything else they claimed to have experienced. This kept me from going off into doc-
trinal extremes.

I always felt there was a peril in seeking just an
experience from the Lord. The temptation is to think
the experience has sanctified. It hasn't. These up-
lifting times in His presence, provings of His faithful care, enrich us, add to our joy, but they do not
sanctify us. They do not make us stronger Christians. They do not make us holier than our fellows,
as I was to learn to my shame. But they do make
us richer in our knowledge of Him, and they give us
joy that addeth no sorrow to it.

The only way to be holy is daily to hand over to the Holy Spirit what Dr. Tozer calls "the hyphenated sins of the human spirit . . . self-righteousness, self-pity, self-confidence, self-admiration, self-love, and a host of others like them . . . which can be removed only in spiritual experience, never by mere instruction. As well try to instruct leprosy out of our system. There must be a work of God in destruction before we are free. *We must invite the Cross to do its deadly work within us. We must bring our self sins to the Cross for judgment."* [1] The Holy Spirit will crucify these things for us, as we hand them over to Him, and then we must accept the suffering involved, rejoicing in the knowledge that His resurrection life will be the final outcome.

And so, with all my rich experience of answered prayers, I was still full of worry, self-pity, and many other ugly things, but I was not acutely conscious they were there.

Mr. Gibb was really perturbed. By now I wore an engagement ring, and John Kuhn was already in China and being used of the Lord there. If my health broke, would that bring John home? Mr. Gibb consulted Mr. Thomson, and they both ordered me to resign from the Corner Club and take six months of complete rest before sailing in October, 1928. Mr. Gibb intended to give instructions that I be put on Mission support in order to do this, but, most unusual for him, he must have forgotten. I waited and waited, but the Mission sent me nothing. And I felt I should not petition them for it. Hudson Taylor would have just prayed.

I forget how it happened, but Mr. and Mrs. Whip-

---

[1] *The Pursuit of God*, by A. W. Tozer.

ple heard of the order for me to rest and invited me to spend the five or six months at The Firs. I could help in cleaning cabins and getting the Conference grounds ready, but first I was to have a full month of nothing but rest—even breakfast in bed!

I had been able to save no money, for I had felt I should pay my father's debts. It was clear to me that the next invention would never bring him an income, and I was right. So I landed at The Firs with about thirty-six dollars—all the money I had left.

No one can know what it meant to me to be taken in by dear cheery Mrs. Whipple, and be given the upstairs porch which they were fixing up as bedroom for their own daughter, Lois, when she should return from the Bible Institute of Los Angeles, where she was studying. Two sides of the room were without full walls and the scented, tall fir trees were its screen. Mrs. Whipple had procured some old cement sacks. These she had bleached, stenciling a pretty fleur-de-lis pattern on them, and hung them up in lieu of walls. When the opening of the conference would bring many people around, and the fir trees might not afford privacy enough, these curtains could be drawn. But when I arrived, the scented green needles were the wall, and I loved it. To wake up in the morning having slept to the full, no pressure of schedule upon me, to hear the birds caroling and the sun trying to peep at me through the green foliage was like living with God in Eden. I can never forget it.

I knew that the Whipples were "living by faith," but had no idea that when they took me in that first night they were down to rock bottom financially. I felt I would like to give them my thirty-six dollars. Before going to bed, I handed the money to her, saying, "I want you to take this. It won't pay for all I'll eat these months, but I'd feel happier if I felt I'd given something."

I remember Mrs. Whipple flushed a bit and tried to refuse, but I insisted, and then the matter left my mind. She told me years afterward that that was one of the hardest things she ever did—to take my money. But the milk bill was due in the morning and she had nothing else with which to meet it. And I myself would need milk. My money fed us until a gift of sixty dollars came in, and from then on there was no shortage. This is just a glimpse of how the Whipples lived: although the gifts had been few, they did not hesitate to invite me to live with them for six months. And I do not need to say how God blessed them.

They had returned from China to find that The Firs was the only home they had. With funds low and the need to make and furnish a bedroom for Lois—and me!—they were put on their mettle. From the attic of a relative they obtained some old furniture free, and this they sandpapered and re-painted a pretty green for Lois's bedroom. When the stenciled curtains were hung, it was as dainty a room as a girl could wish—and I had learned lots about how to convert old things into new!

The Conference that summer (1928) was the most blessed I had ever known. The special speaker was Dr. Arthur Harris of Wales, and the Spirit of the Lord was powerfully among us. For one thing, Mrs. Whipple had prayed that every young person attending the Conference should yield to the Lord before going home. One evening during the service she was impelled to go to the girls' dormitory, and there she knelt by each bed, claiming for Christ the occupant of that bed. Needless to say, every evening there were decisions made. Toward the last evening there were a few who still hung back from full surrender, so the staff called us leaders of the young people to pray all during the evening service. I can never forget that prayer service. The Spirit of the Lord came down upon us as in apostolic times, and we all started to pray simultaneously out loud. As for myself, I was not even conscious of the others. So lifted up was I into the Lord's presence and so burdened for the souls that were hanging back, that it was not until a break came that I suddenly came down to earth and realized that we had all been praying aloud together. From the upper room where we prayed, down through the treetops, we could see the open-air auditorium. As we prayed, one after another of the recalcitrant ones got up and went forward in surrender. The very last, a girl for whom I had held but little hope, has now been for decades a most faithful missionary on a foreign field. Very truly it was the work of the Spirit of God.

Conference over, I needed to go back to Vancouver and get my outfit ready for China. There were still no funds sent to me by the Mission, but a love-gift from my brother paid my fare home. (When Murray saw Dad's invention was not likely to make him rich, he had set about getting a job.) But where would the next money come from? To add to the perplexity came a letter from Marjorie Harrison saying that she was traveling in our parts and would like to stop off and see us. When I answered with a cordial invitation, I did not have enough money to pay her carfare from the station to our home, let alone feed her.

Then I got a call from **Mr. Thomson** to come to his office, as there was some money waiting for me. *At last!* I said jubilantly to myself. Mr. Gibb has remembered his promise! But it was no such thing. It was much more wonderful than that. It was fifty dollars from my own dear John in China! I think it was the remainder of a bank account he had left over from his earnings in preparation for Bible school days. "I want to have a share in your outfit," he wrote, "but it has no strings on it: you may use it for any need." And the first bit of it fed Marjorie!

From then on I had no difficulty. The Corner Club girls gave me showers and a beautiful outfit, which included the money to buy a portable organ. That little organ went with us to the Salween mountains and brought much joy to Lisu as well as to us missionaries for many years.

I prayed much about my final message at the Corner Club. I did not know, though I shrewdly suspected it, that some of those dear girls were going to prove prayer-warriors for whom I would thank the Lord all my missionary days. It has been so now for twenty-eight years. God laid on my heart a message for myself as well as for them from Hebrews 6:1, *Let us go on.*

The search is not ended. We have only begun to explore our eternal, unfathomable God. "Let us leave behind the elementary teaching about Christ and go forward to adult understanding. Let us not lay over and over again the foundation truths. . . . No, if God allows, *let us go on,*" paraphrases Phillips. And that was the burden of my message.

On October 11, 1928, I sailed for China. There was quite a large party of us, one being the little American girl who roomed next to me in Ransom

Hall at Moody Bible Institute: Ella Dieken was engaged to Jack Graham, and we were to be room-mates at the Language School in China. My father had permission to sail with me on our steamer as far as Victoria, so that the emotion of parting from him did not take place at the wharf in Vancouver. The ship was due to pull out about noon, and the Corner Club girls forsook their lunch and flocked down to the wharf. They made such a crowd that a stranger asked my brother, "Who is the girl who is getting this send-off?" Just an unknown missionary going out for the first time, was certainly not the answer expected. But God can give special things to His unknown children when He wants to.

At last a bugler climbed up to the highest bridge of the *Empress of Russia* and began to play Queen Liliuokalani's beautiful farewell song, *Aloha Oe*. It is of course the sad parting of two lovers. It breathes passion, but no certitude of hope. It is earth doing its best to reach out for cheer, but fail-ing mournfully. I am so glad that Christian words have been set to that music for such moments. For it is only Christians who dare to say, "We never part for the *last* time." As the bugle notes poured forth on the noisy air of the wharf, there gradually grew a stillness over the crowd.

> In these the closing days of time
>   What peace this glorious thought affords
> That soon, O wondrous truth sublime,
>   He shall come, King of kings and Lord of lords
>
> He's coming soon, He's coming soon
>   With joy we'll welcome His returning;
> It may be morn, it may be night or noon
>   But oh, He's coming soon.

But "the gospel must first be published among all nations" (Mark 13:10).

And we, who living yet remain
  Caught up shall meet our faithful Lord.
This hope we cherish not in vain
  But we comfort one another with this word.

The last notes quavered sadly on the high air. The unbelieving in the crowd, grasping the only best they knew, whispered, "Aloha Oe." The big anchors rattled as they were pulled up, the paper streamers began to tear as the mighty ship slowly drew away from the wharf. Beloved girl faces were working with emotion, and one or two were crying. "Lord," I whispered, "give me a last word they won't forget." A thrown voice could still reach the wharf. I leaned over the side and called out slowly, *"Let us go on!"*

The light of heaven broke through the tears of earth on some faces, so I knew they had heard. They waved their hands in a signal of assent and then the *Empress of Russia* turned her stately head slowly toward the Narrows, Puget Sound, the Pacific Ocean, and—China.

But there was one more step. At the city of Victoria, on Vancouver Island, my father said good-by and disembarked. After he had left, the purser brought me a telegram. It read simply, WE WILL GO ON—YOUR CORNER CLUB GIRLS.

Tears of gratitude rained in my heart. Twenty-eight years have passed—a good, long testing period. The Corner Club is still operating. Most of those girls have gone on with the Lord. There are people in more than one country of the world who rise up and call some of them blessed. One of them on the wharf that day had unconsciously been leaning on me rather than on the Lord Himself, so she sprawled spiritually when her human prop was removed. But on the whole they kept their promise.

And now, as reader and author part, I can find no better words to use than these same, *"Let us go on."* Go on searching and exploring the greatness and the dearness of our God.

He has no favorites. He has said, "Ye shall find me when ye shall search for me with all your heart" (Jer. 29:13).

Notice that last phrase, for it is the only condition. There must be inner honesty and undivided loyalty—that is the only stipulation. "The man who trusts God, *but with inward reservations,* is like a wave of the sea, carried forward by the wind one moment and driven back the next. That sort of man cannot hope to receive anything from God, and the life of a man *of divided loyalty* will reveal instability at every turn" (Jas. 1:6-8—Phillips thus paraphrases it).

But—"He is a rewarder of them that diligently seek him" (Heb. 11:6).

Said Susanna Wesley, "He is so infinitely blessed, that every perception of His blissful presence imparts a gladness to the heart. Every degree of approach to Him is, in the same proportion, a degree of happiness."

So—*Let us go on*—SEARCHING.